Praise for Ya'Acov Darling Khan and *Shaman*

'Our world is changing faster than we ever thought it could. The danger is immense, but so is the potential for utter – and beautiful – transformation. The strong, true, clear heart that Ya'Acov Darling Khan brings to his work and his writing is one of the things that gives me hope.

In the words of Greta Thunberg, speaking truth to power: "It is no longer enough to be the best that we can be. We need to be better."

And if this book sings to you, as it can, and if you follow every ritual and meditation with integrity and depth and absolute dedication – as you can – then I can promise your world will be a brighter, sharper, more magical place. And you will be on your way to being better than the best you could be.'

MANDA SCOTT, AUTHOR OF THE *BOUDICA* SERIES

'A gentle spirit suffuses this book, which nonetheless brooks no nonsense.'

CHARLES EISENSTEIN, SPEAKER AND AUTHOR OF *THE ASCENT OF HUMANITY*

'Only a truly authentic leader could bring a book titled Shaman into existence, and there is no question that Ya'Acov Darling Khan deserves the honour. Shaman is an invitation not just to the young generation, but to us all. To see our lives as canvasses ready to be made into art. To step up and into our true power and transform some of its most pressing issues. "We are made of star dust" Ya'Acov reminds us, and if we engage with Shaman like the blessed text it is, the possibility of transformation for ourselves and the world we occupy stands before us. May its message travel far and wide.'

JESSICA HUIE MBE, AUTHOR OF *PURPOSE*

'Ya'Acov is a gifted healer of the highest integrity who has written a masterpiece that will help you understand, embrace and harness the power of your Inner Shaman. His words and guidance serve as a path to live with greater purpose and create a world where we can turn suffering into healing. Thank you, Ya'Acov, for being such a blessing, in and for our world.'

VEX KING, MIND COACH AND BESTSELLING AUTHOR OF *GOOD VIBES, GOOD LIFE*

'This book is a magnificent song in praise of life. Deeply insightful, moving and raw, it overflows with Ya'Acov's genuine humility and courageous spirit. I feel this book pulsing with the drumbeat of hope, calling us to find our own Inner Shaman so that together we can birth a new world. I hear Ya'Acov urging us to read and then dance!'

TIM FREKE, AUTHOR OF *DEEP AWAKE* AND *SOUL STORY*

'Shaman is a label that many start using after a weekend workshop and a swig of plant medicine. It took Ya'Acov 30 years of deep study to start using it, and only then after it was asked of him by his indigenous teachers. He has been doing the inner work for a lifetime. You can trust him. His roots are deep and his heart is open. He will sing for you and teach you to remember the words of your own song too.'

CHARLIE MORLEY, LUCID DREAMING TEACHER AND
BESTSELLING AUTHOR OF *DREAMS OF AWAKENING*

'This is a book with a compelling and timely message, delivered with a warm-hearted and down-to-earth kind of magic that reminds you of what you've always known deep down, but maybe forgot. There's no doubt we're in a time of tumultuous change, with a global call of "All hands on deck!" for anyone who will hear it. Ya'Acov is definitely on deck, and I'm glad to have his strong voice alongside, encouraging and calling for more.'

ADAM BARLEY, ZEROONE MOVEMENT PRACTICE FOUNDER

'Ya'Acov moves with the times and uses modern concepts such as archetypes to offer shamanism to today's people in the Western world. With the power of his intent and dedication, Ya'Acov stands today as a guide and pathfinder for people who are looking to deepen their connection with earth, spirit and their true self.'

CHRIS LUTTICHAU, NORTHERN DRUM SHAMANIC CENTRE, AUTHOR OF *CALLING US HOME*

'Ya'Acov is a shaman of strong words and deep intention. He always has been and always will be. He knows that thoughts and words become things. In his latest book, Shaman, he reaches all of us with his clear congruent communication. His words clarify the journey, and with his contemporary, embodied practice he has manifested a creative empowered framework that eases some of the road ahead. The sweetness and dignity of his words will fortify the worlds of your own becoming.'

KATE SHELA, 360 EMERGENCE MOVEMENT PRACTICE FOUNDER

'Ya'Acov is the real deal, and he's doing incredibly sacred work that the world needs more than ever. Let him guide you deep into the truth of who you are.'

KYLE GRAY, BESTSELLING AUTHOR OF *ANGEL PRAYERS* AND *RAISE YOUR VIBRATION*

'I have been married to Ya'Acov for over three decades. He is my best friend and much more besides. We have shared so many ups and downs as we learned, loved, fought and brought our work into the world. Over the years, as we have met indigenous groups in different places round the world, over and over again the same thing has happened: out of the blue, elder shamans recognized him and told us that he is a shaman too. These were people who knew nothing about him and who did not have anything to gain from recognizing him in this way. They simply saw who he is.

I'm proud to stand by his side and uphold him, his integrity and this amazing book. It makes clear what a genuine and inspiring shamanic practice, relevant to the wounds, challenges and opportunities of our modern world, can mean.'

SUSANNAH DARLING KHAN

'It is tough owning being a shaman if you haven't grown up in an indigenous tribe in the Amazon. Ya'Acov has not only managed this for himself, in this book he shows how you can contact the essence of shamanism for yourself.'

PROFESSOR JAKE CHAPMAN, AUTHOR, ENLIGHTENMENT MASTER AND CLIMATE ACTIVIST FOR 50 YEARS

'I've known Ya'Acov Darling Khan for 29 years. He's a powerful medicine man who walks the talk. In these divisive times we need the shamans' teachings more than ever, to come together, to face the extinction crisis that threatens this life we are all dreaming together.'

TIM BOOTH, LEAD SINGER, JAMES

'None of us can tell quite what even the near future holds, yet a growing mass of us sense that this Great Shift is away from the heady and the mechanistic and towards the immanent and the earthbound – towards a more embodied humanity; towards the shamanic. A great awakening is needed, that much is clear, and addressing this, and doing so as directly and practically as you have, Ya'Acov, makes this book a vital transmission in these times. I am grateful!'

NICK MULVEY, SINGER-SONGWRITER, ACTIVIST AND MERCURY MUSIC PRIZE NOMINEE

'Ya'Acov is providing, through his life experience, a dance for us to step into that can return us to source, and make sense of the cacophonous, disingenuous noise competing for our attention in the everyday. He is reminding us of the dark dance of individualized presence and exploration that is necessary for all to come together in collective resonance to illuminate our inherent power.'

VINN ARJUNA, FOUNDER OF SOUL MOTION

'Ya'Acov invites us to discover the power, purpose and presence that the archetype of the Inner Shaman already has access to. Shaman offers a clearly guided, grounded and embodied road to encounter this ancient archetype and apply its wisdom, not just to our own lives, but in relationship to the wider story in which we all exist.'

BILL AND LYNNE TWIST, CO-FOUNDERS, THE PACHAMAMA ALLIANCE

'I have travelled along a synergetic path with Ya'Acov Darling Khan for many years and have observed his connection with spirit and ceremony deepen as he has developed his mastery as a teacher, wisdom-keeper and shaman. His words and teachings will connect you with your own shamanic source and bring you into your authentic self, ready to create the new dream.'

LYNNE FRANKS OBE, FOUNDER OF THE SEED WOMEN'S NETWORK

'Shamanism is, foremost, the practice of understanding one's physical and spiritual environment. In our time, we need shamans who are rooted in the modern world and who also have their spiritual roots in shamanic traditions. As you are guided by Ya'Acov towards a deeper wholeness, you will understand that although the forms of rituals change when the environment changes, the true essence of shamanism is present in each of his teachings.'

DAAN VAN KAMPENHOUT, SHAMAN AND AUTHOR OF *THE TEARS OF THE ANCESTORS*

'We need to bring solutions to these times of trouble and change, and I thank my brother Ya'Acov for the work he has done to put into written form the ancient memories of our ancestors. May this work touch many hearts and bring a light of understanding to the young and all those who are available to receive it. The spirit of the shaman lives on in the deepest places of our heart as a collective treasure that we all cherish and share as spirits in human bodies.'

MAO TATANKA, SHAMAN

SHAMAN

Also by Ya'Acov Darling Khan

Books

Jaguar in the Body, Butterfly in the Heart: The Real-Life Initiation of an Everyday Shaman (Hay House, 2017)

Movement Medicine: How to Awaken, Dance and Live Your Dreams
Ya'Acov and Susannah Darling Khan (Hay House, 2009)

Audio products

Shaman's Song: Shamanic Journeys to Empower, Inspire and Reconnect
Ya'Acov and Susannah Darling Khan
and Friends (Hay House, 2018)

Movement Meditation Volume 1: For the Dance of Life
Ya'Acov and Susannah Darling Khan
and Friends (Hay House, 2009)

SHAMAN

Invoking Power, Presence and Purpose
at the Core of Who You Are

YA'ACOV DARLING KHAN

HAY HOUSE

Carlsbad, California • New York City
London • Sydney • New Delhi

Published in the United Kingdom by:
Hay House UK Ltd, The Sixth Floor, Watson House
54 Baker Street, London W1U 7BU
Tel: +44 (0)20 3927 7290; Fax: +44 (0)20 3927 7291
www.hayhouse.co.uk

Published in the United States of America by:
Hay House Inc., PO Box 5100, Carlsbad, CA 92018-5100
Tel: (1) 760 431 7695 or (800) 654 5126
Fax: (1) 760 431 6948 or (800) 650 5115; www.hayhouse.com

Published in Australia by:
Hay House Australia Ltd, 18/36 Ralph St, Alexandria NSW 2015
Tel: (61) 2 9669 4299; Fax: (61) 2 9669 4144; www.hayhouse.com.au

Published in India by:
Hay House Publishers India, Muskaan Complex,
Plot No.3, B-2, Vasant Kunj, New Delhi 110 070
Tel: (91) 11 4176 1620; Fax: (91) 11 4176 1630; www.hayhouse.co.in

Text © Ya'Acov Darling Khan, 2020
Illustrations © Ya'Acov and Susannah Darling Khan, 2020

The information given in this book should not be treated as a substitute for professional medical advice; always consult a medical practitioner. Any use of information in this book is at the reader's discretion and risk. Neither the author nor the publisher can be held responsible for any loss, claim or damage arising out of the use, or misuse, of the suggestions made, the failure to take medical advice or for any material on third-party websites.

A catalogue record for this book is available from the British Library.

ISBN: 978-1-4019-6080-3
E-book ISBN: 978-1-78817-256-1
Audiobook ISBN: 978-1-78817-384-1

Interior illustrations created by Ed Price

Printed in the United States of America

*I dedicate this book to the dream that we will turn
the corner, mature as a species and use our massive
ingenuity to protect life rather than destroy it.
For our children, the generations that will
follow and for all our relations.*

Contents

List of Practices

Foreword

I met Ya'Acov in 2011 when he and his wife, Susannah, came to visit my village, Llanchamacocha. They were travelling with their colleague David Tucker from the Pachamama Alliance and a group of people from around the world. They came not as tourists, but as allies of the forest.

The forest has been the home of my people, the Sápara, for millennia. We do not own it, or the land; we are not superior to the earth, rivers or trees. Our lives are based on recognizing the sacredness of all things – animate, inanimate and even invisible. We believe that everything that lives has a spirit and that we can all make direct connections with the spirit world through dreams. We are all potentially equal strands with a part to play in the web of life. We envision a world in which society understands the importance of living in harmony with the Earth and the rights of nature are respected by all. Our fight to protect the Amazon before it disappears is a fight that belongs to us all.

There are now fewer than 600 of my people left and only five of us still speak the Sápara language. We are aware we could disappear from the world completely in the near future. Yet we still have something unique to offer and we are committed to sharing our knowledge of medicinal plants and the spirit world for the benefit of all peoples. So I was honoured to meet Ya'Acov and the group travelling with him.

The night before he arrived, we met in our dreaming. Ya'Acov came and stood outside my house and sang. I recognized his song and my father, a well-known and powerful shaman who passed away some years ago, came to meet him and took us into the forest, where we met three jaguars. I meet my father every night when I dream and that night he showed me that Ya'Acov was an ally for me and for our people. I knew then that Ya'Acov and I were brothers.

Over the years, we have worked together in my village and in the UK, where every year I join Ya'Acov and Susannah's Long Dance ceremony. So I have come to know him both as a friend and as a very genuine and compassionate shaman. He has put his knowledge in the service of healing through music, sound and movement, and leads very powerful ceremonies that transform thousands of people, helping them to deal with their suffering and answer their most important questions. He is a great healer who has helped me in my shamanic spiritual growth.

Ya'Acov and Susannah often show up in our ceremonies and our dreams. They bring healing and we call on their strength when we work with our medicine ceremonies. Ya'Acov is always there when we need him, helping us to keep the oil in the ground and protecting the community and the river with shields and spirits. There have been many other powerful signs of our connection and our work together.

And we are there for him and his family and the people they work with. Our collaboration is part of an ancient prophecy that says that the way we will come through the challenges we are now facing as a species is to connect across cultures. We need to bring together the best of what we all know in order to find solutions to our collective challenges. We share one Earth and we must remember that we need each other.

We believe that the people of the modern world need to wake up and connect with their natural and ancestral vision and activate their tribal knowledge to live through these times with less disease of the body and disease of the spirit. It is important to rediscover our collective ancestral heritage and to remember the archetype of the Shaman. Ya'Acov's book, like everything he does, is full of power straight from the heart. When he speaks, it is a direct transmission from the spirits to whom he is connected, including the spirits of the forest. I am certain that this book will bring you inspiration, help you to remember what you already know deep inside yourself and open the door between the worlds of the sleeping and the waking dream.

The practices that Ya'Acov is sharing with you are strong medicine and they will support you in making or deepening your connection to the Inner Shaman. This part of you remembers who you are, who your people and your guides are, what you are connected to, and what your work is. They are also tuned in to the spirit guides of the forest and the universe. They can show you the changes you need to make in your life in relationship to yourself, others, the community of life, your ancestors and guides and the source of life itself, so that future generations can survive and thrive in this world.

I am longing to continue working in collaboration with my brother Ya'Acov, uniting the spirits and shamanic knowledge. My father's spirit, my community and I hold him and his work in deep respect and affection. May this book reach all those who need to be touched by its wisdom. And may you feel the transmission of the ancient spirits through this modern understanding of how shamanism and the Inner Shaman can inspire and help you in your day-to-day life.

Witsaha. Thank you.

Manari Kaji Ushigua Santi
Shaman and leader of the Sápara nation
of the Amazon rainforest of Ecuador

21 Gratitudes

1. I am grateful to have this opportunity to thank the community of souls who brought this book into existence.

2. The first person I want to thank is my wife, Susannah. You looked after me with such grace, surrender and beauty for the two intense summers of ritual that writing this book was for me. Without your love and support with this and over more than three decades of marriage, your belief in me, the love made visible in your cooking, care and in our work, the touch of your hands, and the bright intelligence of who you are, I would not manage 20 per cent of what I am able to offer this world. Thank you. I bow at the doorway between us.

3. Just in case anyone's worried about my beloved getting a raw deal, don't worry, folks, it's my turn next. I am grateful that next time, it will be my honour to do the same for her so that she can write the book that's bursting to come through her.

4. To our son, Reuben. To have you at my back is such a support. And it's my privilege to be at your back too. The way we are father and son together is a revolution. This book is a prayer for you and all your companions.

5. Thanks, Mum. You're a shining star, a genuinely faithful angel, and you matter more than you know.

6. To my father, thank you. You played your role perfectly in my life. I wish I'd known then what I know now.

7. To my beautiful sisters, Sharon and Lisa, thank you for being you. I've been far away much of the time, but you are always in my heart.

8. The same can be said for my whole family. I am so proud of you all.

9. And to my ancestors, who survived so much and who bravely passed life on, your songs and dances are in my heart.

10. Thank you to Michelle Pilley for suggesting I write this. Gratitude number 10 goes to you and all the crew at Hay House for your ongoing support over many years.

11. I only recently discovered what an extraordinary woman Louise Hay was and I am super grateful to her for her life and for the dream she made manifest called Hay House, through which I can send this book into the world.

12. A big thank-you to Nikki Van de Car, whose Hawaiian soul gave the much-needed second writing of this book so much more life, clarity and focus. My thanks to you and your people.

13. Lizzie Henry, what a warrior you are. Your editing is sharp, precise and kind. I love your humour and I am so glad you came back from the edge to offer what's so natural to you and so helpful to me and so many more. Thank you!

14. Roland Wilkinson, trustworthy friend and business partner over so many years – your service to us and to our community is a legend. Thank you.

15. There are many people all around the world who organize my events and who have done so over the past three decades. Your commitment, your care for the details and the people, and the generosity of your work is overwhelming. Thank you.

16. To the seven generations of Movement Medicine apprentices, all of you, without exception, thank you for demanding the best of me. May all of you come to know who you truly are and receive all you need to continue bringing your dreams to Earth.

17. To all my teachers, most especially Bikko Máhte Penta, Gabrielle Roth and the elders in the forest. Your shaman's shoulders are mighty to stand on and your teachings live in my heart. It's my intention always to honour you, develop what you have given me and pass it on far and wide.

18. To the spirit of the dance, no words, just boom shaka boom!

19. To all the spirits, the elementals, the invisibles, the spirits of the land on which I live, thanks for your patience. Another day, another step.

20. My thanks to you, dear reader, for picking this up and diving in. And to the Inner Shaman in you for reminding you that, like it or not, we are all, without exception, in this together. For the love of life.

21. Creator, Great Spirit, holy mama, holy papa, if only we could know who we are. Thank you.

Introduction

My name is Ya'Acov Darling Khan. I am a shaman. I didn't give myself the title; it was given to me. Traditionally, the title of shaman is never claimed by an individual, but is given to them by their teachers, elders and community. What I found was that for many years I had the same experience over and over again: without knowing me, and often without previous conversations, indigenous elders and shamans recognized me as a colleague. More recently, they have trusted me to work with members of their own families and communities. But, as a white man in the modern world, it has taken me nearly three decades to fully understand and accept the role of shaman.

On the one hand, being a shaman is simply a job, or perhaps more accurately a vocation. On the other hand, it takes decades of intense learning to embody the role. It's one of those jobs where you get better the older and more experienced you get. It is a lifelong invitation to serve the systemic wellbeing of the community, human and non-human, physical and non-physical.

After I shared the story of my shamanic initiation in my last book, *Jaguar in the Body, Butterfly in the Heart* (Hay House, 2017), I had a meeting with Michelle, managing director and publisher at Hay House UK, to discuss what I could offer next in book form. She told me that, surprisingly, no one had yet written a book simply called *Shaman*, and asked if I would write one to offer my perspective on the role of the shaman and the use of shamanism in the modern world. She knew that my wife, Susannah, and I had dedicated our lives to creating a body of work that had shamanism at its heart.

I thought long and hard about writing such a book. I knew it would be a challenge to do justice to such a huge and complex subject. And I also recognized the issues surrounding cultural appropriation that are rightly coming more into awareness. Though Susannah and I have studied with and been inspired by many indigenous teachers, our work is not taken from these traditions, but there is no getting away from the reality that I am a privileged white man. To be accurate, I am 92.4 per cent Ashkenazi Jewish, the great-grandson of Eastern European refugees. I am also 1.5 per cent Greek, 1.2 per cent West Asian, 1.2 per cent North African and 0.9 per cent Inuit. I can also say that shamanism has been my passion from the moment I discovered its existence shortly after being struck by lightning in my early twenties.

So, I sat with Michelle's invitation for some time and then I did what shamans do: I went into ceremony and prayed for guidance. This book is the result of the guidance I received. Having said that, it isn't about me. It's about you. It's about us and where we are as a species. It's an invocation to a powerful archetypal energy, the Inner Shaman, which is in us all. It's a call to that Shaman to awaken. The Inner Shaman is a healer and stands at the doorway between what we dream and how we live, reminding us of our responsibility to the truth inside us and to the health of the whole web of life.

As we step forward on this journey, it feels important to me to acknowledge that *shaman* is a word with a deeply sacred and deeply painful history. Throughout human history, shamans have been women, men, gender fluid, people of colour and white of skin. The massive damage that the European colonizers did to the indigenous peoples and traditions of the world was first seen in Europe itself, where the Roman Catholic Church and the Spanish Inquisition destroyed the native shamanic traditions without mercy and with diabolical violence. In Europe, we cut down our forests and then set out to export this story of 'civilization' around the world through the horrors and dogmatic marriage of Church and empire. And though the genocide of indigenous peoples and their traditions is well documented, it is far from healed.

It's no wonder that there are many within the indigenous traditions of the world who feel further betrayed by the ways in which their shamanic practices have been consistently and unconsciously appropriated without permission. At the same time, there are many within those traditions whose guidance has inspired them to share their wisdom in order to remind the people of the industrialized world of what is sacred before it is too late for us all.

Shamanism in the modern world, like most other subjects, is a multi-layered and complex landscape, and I fully understand why people may question my use of the word *shaman*. As I explained earlier, I am using it because shamans from the Amazon to the Arctic have asked me to carry it and take something of its Unbroken spirit back to my own land and people. One of my central teachers was 'urban shaman' Gabrielle Roth, a New Yorker in a black leather jacket with a heart full of incisive, street-wise and challenging truths. She urged Susannah and me to give ourselves to the beat, lose ourselves to the dance and mend the split between body and spirit. Our work with her was the high-intensity cauldron in which, over 18 years of apprenticeship, we discovered our own work. And she was very clear that although we can learn a lot from shamans and teachers from other cultures, *shamanism is indigenous to its own culture.*

Whatever their culture, shamans have certain things in common. For example, they speak for the invisible realms. They speak for the non-human worlds. They remind us of our responsibility to be caretakers of the future through our choices in the present. And for that reason, the return of shamanism and its evolution in the modern world matter a great deal. In itself, this would have been enough reason for me to agree to write this book. Added to it is the fact that western or neo-shamanism often appears to have more to do with status, exotic appropriated fashion items and otherworldly experiences than with the very real work of healing and living with awareness of and care for one another and our environment.

Susannah and I have dedicated our lives to integrating, distilling and offering the essential medicine we have learned from our studies around the world, including within our own culture. Early on, our indigenous teachers taught us that it was our job to adapt what we had learned for our own culture, and that is exactly what we have done. The shamanic practice I'm going to share with you in this book is the result of that. It is an embodied practice, and though it is rooted in ancient wisdom, it is a new and contemporary form. It's called Movement Medicine. Movement Medicine doesn't require costumes, feathers, plant medicines or anything else taken or received from other traditions. It simply invites you to be present in your body, unafraid of your heart and open in your mind. It asks you to take responsibility for who you are, where you come from and what is yours to offer in this world. It doesn't ask you to believe in anything. It does invite you to trust the power of your embodied imagination.

The title of this book is an invocation. And I am drumming and singing it into the eight directions, through the roots, trunk and branches of the Tree of Life: '*Shaman!* Hey! You there! Yes, you! I'm calling to you – you inside your skin, inside your bones. To the ancient memories that are alive in your DNA – the Inner Shaman who remembers your unbreakable connection to the magnificent spirit of life and who you truly are. It's time to awaken. Your body needs you. The Earth needs you. Your heart needs you. Your dreams need you. You are creation itself in the form of a human, and you have so much to give…'

My intention is to show you that there is an Inner Shaman within you, an archetype that I believe has a powerful role to play in the personal and collective awakening we need to engage in if we are to have a future on Earth. Some say it is already too late for us. But my own experience tells me that we have barely begun to understand the power and intelligence of life itself and the potential power of transformation that is within us, between us and between we humans and the web of life. At the end of this book, you will find a way to be in touch with me and share your experience and your feedback. Every shaman I know is hungry to go on learning, and I am no exception.

Human beings are storytellers and meaning makers. The Inner Shaman reminds us that we each have the power to weave the best of all stories into a magnificent tapestry that dignifies who we truly are. And collectively, through a reciprocal and mutually enhancing relationship with nature and the vast Mystery in which we exist, we have the power to create heaven on Earth.

And yet here we are, standing on the brink of catastrophe, still deciding whether we wish to follow our greed and immaturity to their natural conclusion. Will we wake up and take responsibility for what we are dreaming? Will we learn to receive what life is giving us or will we consume ourselves to death? A shaman speaks the language of interconnection. They remind us of the rhythm of life that is dancing inside us and they invite us to follow it. They hold open the doors between the worlds, urging us to realize our power and to use it choice-fully.

Life has been evolving on Earth for 4.5 billion years. And although shamanism has been with us since the dawn of our existence, many of us have been persuaded that its time is over. On the other hand, we are seeing a rise in the pop shamanism of weekend trainings and a lack of professional standards. All this has given the shaman a bad name. But I know in my bones that the Inner Shaman can help us take the opportunities of this time and meet the challenges we face with the same creativity and ingenuity that helped us evolve in the first place. And I am passionate about helping you to get to know and work with the wisdom, power and love for life that the Inner Shaman has brought into my own life and the lives of those with whom I work.

This book is dedicated to our son Reuben's generation and the generations that will follow. Like every previous generation before them, those brave young adults who are waking up to the mix of mess and magnificence we are faced with and the opportunities we all have to do something about it are being stretched beyond what has been known before. I'm told that's called *evolution*.

I am 55 years old and just taking my seat as a young elder. I have learned how to accept my faults and find the dignity to do something about them. I have often leaped off the edge of the known with my arms wide open, shouting with all my heart: 'Bring it on!' I have loved one woman for more than three decades and continue to deepen my love for her. Making shamanism relevant to the 21st century and sharing it as widely as possible is my passion. I love this life. I love my woman. I love our son and I love the land we live on. I am totally attached. And if this is all an illusion, then so be it. I intend to enjoy it for as long as I can. I know my death. And I have seen the death of this Earth and this sun. And of everything I know and everything I don't. And because of that, I follow the total imperative of life's longing to create and create again. As long as my heart is beating, I will praise life, and praise the divine spark that brings life to everything.

I experience life as an ongoing miracle. All of this was once nothing. And inside that nothing was everything that has ever breathed its first and its last breath. We are all made of star dust. Our very bones are made of the material that exploded into being nearly 14 billion years ago.

The work I am inviting you into is knowing yourself as you are: the Great Mystery, developing its knowledge of what this existence is, in the form of *you*. If you so choose, you can awaken and receive this mantle. You can stand up and dance and become proud of who you are. You have travelled a long way to get here. We all have. And this life is sacred. In the most down-to-earth ways we can imagine and in the most psychedelic visions we can design.

And yet, even though we have conquered many of our external challenges as a species through the brilliance of the scientific mind, many of us seem to be suffering from a loss of connection, meaning, purpose, tribe and land that has us racing around in a waking nightmare in which we consume more and more in a desperate attempt to experience life. And the more we consume, the less we feel. Why? Because our body, heart and mind have become fragmented. Our mind by itself is lost. Our heart by itself is overwhelmed. And our body is left to deal with the consequences. Most of us haven't found anything approaching satisfaction through our modern way of life. If we had, perhaps the shaman could continue to hang out on the margins of our global village. But the material success that a growing number of the world's population has enjoyed has brought two major problems: 1) it hasn't delivered the happiness it promised; 2) it has led to us trashing nature's wild beauty in order to feed our growing population and continue the dominant story of our times, which demands material growth.

The Inner Shaman

The universal archetype of the Inner Shaman carries much of the medicine needed to cure the emergent challenges of our times. They are the part of us who knows all the wounds – personal, ancestral and of the time – that we are carrying. They also know the medicine that will transform those challenges into high-octane fuel for living life in a way that honours what truly matters to us.

Your Inner Shaman recognizes your place in the web of life. They are in touch with the indigenous wisdom of your people and your land. They honour your lineage and ancestors and are aware of your responsibility to the generations that will come after you. They recognize the importance of the cycles of life and understand the connection between how you imagine the world to be and how it is. My purpose here is to introduce you to this part of yourself or, if you already know them well, to support you in deepening your relationship.

You don't have to be special to make use of what this archetype can bring you. I am confident that any human being in the modern world, whatever their gender, sexual orientation, religion, colour, culture, belief system or economic status, may benefit greatly from discovering, engaging with and deepening their awareness of this part of themselves. The Inner Shaman is a here and now archetype who knows that things of value take time to grow. They know that in order to harvest the fruit of knowing your place and purpose in life, you have to prepare the soil, plant the seeds and then care for them. In order to manifest a vision, you have to embrace the power you have. And in order to embrace your power safely, you have to find your courage and be prepared to meet and work with a few shadows along the way. Worry not. This book will support you in connecting to the resources, creativity, strength and resilience that the Inner Shaman offers every one of us.

The Inner Shaman knows that the Earth is alive and that our destiny is bound up with hers. They know that life is a gift that is not to be taken for granted. They know that working with the dynamic balance of life rather than attempting to control it has become crucial if we are to evolve as a species. Like it or not, we have created a scenario where we must either become caretakers of the ecosystem that sustains all life on Earth or we must accept that life may have to move on without us, or at least without a lot of us. The evolution of the modern shaman, the return of shamanism to the industrialized world and the growth of interest in shamanic practice are some of our ways of remembering our place in the web of life, our dependency on it and our responsibility to it.

The Inner Shaman recognizes the importance of becoming conscious of how we are bringing our visions to Earth. We do this in so many tiny ways every day and every night, and we can determine whether we do it consciously or continue to act out the deeply held unexamined assumptions that populate our unconscious. So for the Inner Shaman, our connection to the bigger picture translates into simple everyday choices and actions that are congruent with who we choose to be and what we wish to create.

The Inner Shaman also remembers that there is genuinely something missing from modern life. They recognize loss of soul in themselves and others, and the need for healing. They don't shy away from the loneliness in the human spirit and the lack of inspiring meaning and purpose that is ever more evident in our modern world. They know that this lack, and the ever-growing number of distractions designed to keep us from recognizing it, is dangerous for the web of life. They see that many of us are imprisoned in the story that our perception of reality is reality itself. They remember that this means we have a choice. More than that, we are responsible for our choices – not about what happens outside us, but about how we dance as creatively as possible with whatever life brings us. The Inner Shaman weeps often, overwhelmed by the tragedy of it all, but laughs just as often at the searing intensity and paradoxes of life in a body. They are untamed. They remember and embody the magnificent sensuality of life in a body. They are an elemental, solar-powered blend of animal and human, exquisite sensitivity and raw power. They know the ecstasy of surrender to a higher power. They know how to surrender to the rhythm, disappear in the dance and bring back inspiration and strength for the tribe.

The Unbroken

The Inner Shaman stands on the bridge between what I call 'the Unbroken' and the broken. The Unbroken is that spirit in life and in us that remains whole. Whatever your experience of life so far, if your heart is still beating then the Unbroken is alive and well inside you. At the same time, we all carry the challenges and wounds of what has been broken in us, in our families and in our cultures. The Inner Shaman reminds us of the one whilst helping us to work with the other so that we can continue to be part of the evolutionary arc of life on Earth. How? Through the practice of ritual.

A ritual is a time to expand our view and see the bigger picture our story is part of. It is a time to acknowledge challenges, give thanks, grieve and celebrate. It's a time to connect to the Unbroken and surrender to the higher power we trust most, so that we can be healed, strengthened and instructed. In ritual, we remember the things that matter most to us and we strengthen our commitment to them. Ritual returns us to the core, to the humming intelligence of life within all life, and to the source that powers it all. During our journey, I am going to share with you the principles and practices that I have found useful in developing the art of ritual.

Everyday Engaged Shamanism

When ritual ends is when everyday engaged shamanism really begins. The Inner Shaman understands how to plant the seeds of their vision in the fertile ground that is the ongoing miracle of everyday life. They understand how past trauma affects us in the present and how potency comes from transforming that past. They know that the future isn't something that's going to happen to us but something we're going to create together. They understand the law of reciprocity and the dynamic balance of giving and taking. They know that our survival depends on recognizing and taking responsibility for the effect we are having on that dynamic balance. They know the connection between what we imagine and how things turn out. They recognize the power of the free will we are given on this planet. And they are ready to help us harness that power and use it for the greater good.

We humans seem to change when we have to. So maybe our current crisis is the perfect scenario in which to wake up, become aware of the choices we are making and make better ones. We have created the crisis; it is up to us to turn it into an opportunity. Every year, more and more medicine people are emerging from the surviving indigenous traditions of our world to remind us of some of the basics that we are in danger of losing in our rush to 'progress'. They are also quick to pick up on those aspects of our development that may help them and their communities. Our good friend Domingo Paez, a respected elder of the Achuar people of the Ecuadorian Amazon, has made it very clear that if we are to evolve, we have to make use of all of our human ingenuity.

For those in the modern world who are called to this work, shamanism isn't about hanging out on the margins of society, eyes rolled back in constant trance. Genuine shamans are quietly powerful, down-to-earth, humble servants of their communities. They are engaged in the physical world and in touch with the non-physical world for the benefit of all life.

All shamans are human beings, with their own brilliance and shadows. Amongst the surviving indigenous traditions and the growing band of neo-shamanic traditions, as in all areas of life, there are unscrupulous people who will use their power for their own benefit or to do harm. There are charlatans jumping on the bandwagon of shamanism's re-emergence. And there are also many people who have studied deeply and are totally committed to empowering those with whom they work. As with everything, discernment is required.

Our family and friends in the Amazon rainforest have asked us to stand alongside them as they give their lives to protecting the lungs of the Earth. They have asked as many of us as possible to work in our own cultures to 'change the dream of the modern world'. This book is firmly rooted in that intent. To change a dream, you first have to become aware of what you are dreaming, and the best channel I know for that is to invoke the Inner Shaman.

In an age where adventure has been relegated to vicariously living it out on tiny screens, shamanism holds a key to the joy and power of living in a body with heart and soul, engaging passionately with the creative project called a life. Working with the Inner Shaman can help us all to engage passionately with the project of dreaming into being a new chapter for life on Earth, a chapter in which more and more of us learn to work together for the greater good – mystics and mathematicians, shamans and scientists, therapists and surgeons, the apparently rational and the apparently irrational. Each tribe and each perspective holds a piece of the truth.

I've learned many things along the road, but there really is a simple truth in the cliché that the more we know, the more we realize we don't know. Apparently the Mayans had a thing about writing knowledge down and sharing it. They reckoned it was like pouring out the cup of their soul onto the page so that they could become empty again and learn some more. My cup is full. So here I go.

You ready? Let's dance...

Ya'Acov Darling Khan

December 2019

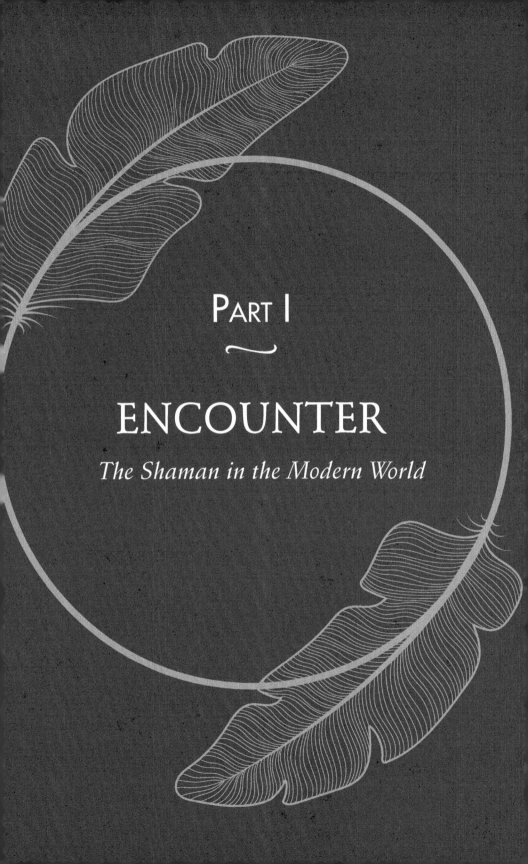

PART I

ENCOUNTER

The Shaman in the Modern World

'We sometimes encounter people, even perfect strangers, who begin to interest us at first sight, somehow, suddenly, all at once, before a word has been spoken.'

FYODOR DOSTOEVSKY

S hamans have always used what's available to them to bring their particular blend of practicality and out-of-the-box invention to their communities. In today's world, the Inner Shaman has the added task of discovering how to combine ancient knowledge with modern understanding of what it takes to transform individual and collective trauma into medicine. This is the bridge across time the Inner Shaman must cross. So, the tools of a modern shaman are just as likely to be a laptop and a playlist as they are to be a drum and beautifully beaded feathers. I like both.

In my work, I have been privileged to witness many thousands of individuals, from many places, cultures and mindsets, bravely struggling to see past their own deep conditioning and rediscover the magnificence, creativity and kindness of their own soul. This has left me with the belief that the shamanic practices that we use in Movement Medicine and that I will share with you in the chapters that follow will be well known to the Shaman in you. I believe that the Earth is crying out for us to remember what we already know.

Modern scientific insight has now converged with ancient shamanic wisdom to reveal that the universe is a complex and interdependent system. This revelation is changing our understanding of the physical world and our place in it. We know there is bad news. The media seems to revel in it. But there is good news too. For the first time in the history of our species, we are engaged in a global conversation about the wrongs of war, inequality, slavery, racism, the abuse of power and the pandemic of sexual abuse. We are becoming aware of a whole host of injustices. We are waking up to the mass extinction our way of our life is causing. The current climate, both political and weather wise, is catalysing us to challenge our apathy and look for new solutions. The study of epigenetics is revealing that we carry both the strength and resilience of our ancestors and their undigested experience. Einstein warned us that we cannot use the same paradigm that created a problem to create the solution. So we know we need inspiration. We need to expand our consciousness if we are to break the chains of suffering and pass on a more evolved story to those who come next.

This has been true for me and I have seen the same in every one of the thousands of people I have worked with over the years. As I grew up, left the relatively safe confines of my own tribe and ventured out into the world, I began to question some of the things I had taken for granted. My thirst for knowledge, a meeting with death when I was struck by lightning on a golf course in my early twenties and the connection to spirit I'd had for as long as I could remember led me on a 30-year initiatory journey from neurotic young Jewish warrior to the shaman that my teachers were telling me I was.

I described in my last book how I came to accept that role. In this one I am inviting you to experience for yourself just how powerful the Inner Shaman can be in your life. In this first part I will give you the basic practices to prepare the ground for your first encounter with them. Later, we will go much deeper, but please don't underestimate the importance of the early stages. Shamanism is powerful work, and in the modern world you need to be embodied and present in order to make proper use of whatever the Inner Shaman may show you. I have found that a good grasp of the basics is worth its weight in gold when you get to the deeper and more challenging work to which your healing will inevitably bring you. The more attention you give to the foundations, the further you will go.

When Susannah and I got together, we discovered very early on that we had a shared mission. Simply put, we wanted to find or create a body of work that supported all who engaged with it to heal their relationship with themselves, with others, with the Earth and the community of life, with ancestors, descendants and spirits, and with the power to consciously create with life and the Creator.

At the centre of our practice and study is a contemporary shamanic ritual that has taken place each year for the past decade. It's called the Summer Long Dance. The Long Dance is a contemporary shamanic fusion of everything we have learned and the alchemy that it rests in is the marriage of ancient and modern shamanism that infuses our work, much of which I intend to share with you in this book. The ritual is a mending of what has been lost, but it is also a stepping into the here and now. It's a place to grieve and a place to dream. It holds at its heart the prayer that we can come through our current challenges and change the dream of life on Earth. It gives those present the opportunity to dedicate their considerable power to serving life as well as receiving all that it has to offer. This is modern shamanism, and the power of this ceremony, and all the work I offer, is rooted in the basic practices I will share with you here.

Modern shamanic practice is a space for your indigenous self, the part of you that remembers your connection to matter and to spirit, the part of you that is unafraid to let the rhythm take you, shake you until you're empty and then lift your heart towards the Mystery. It's a place in which to acknowledge the pain in the world, and inside yourself, and to gain the resources to do something about it, a place where prayer doesn't mean 'believing in' but 'being in direct relationship with', a place where you can honour your ancestors and listen to the dreams of descendants yet to be born.

The practices I am going to share with you will invite you to enter the unknown. We won't use drugs or plant medicine. But you will connect to the intelligence of your body, heart and mind. You will be invited to discover the medicine that is in your past and be given tools to help you be more present and call in and embody inspiration for the future. You will meet your ancestors and discover the powerful effect your imagination is already having on your life. Healing will come, and I have every confidence that you will discover more of your potential to be yourself and make a difference in this world. My spirits tell me that an awakening is happening and that everyone is invited.

I want you to know just how powerful, creative and healing contemporary shamanism can be. Imagine a huge white tent in a field, with a decorated Tree of Life at the centre and 200 people dancing to the shamanic fusion soundscape of drums, guitar, sax, piano and didge. We've been dancing for three days already and many of us have been fasting too. There's a super strong and exquisite Movement Medicine woman (that's my sweetheart) conducting the band, translating the alchemy of the moment into sound to help the dancers let go. There's a Sápara shaman (that's my brother Manari) sitting in prayer, whistling the melodies of the forest into the mix. To my right, our son, Reuben, and his brother Jonas, bring in the medicine they've been gathering on their own paths and add young jaguar energy to the ceremony. And I'm there on my feet, singing out my heart as we shed tears and sweat our prayers late into the night.

Imagine now the luminous quiet that descends so sweetly after the storm. We are all bathed in the sweet nectar of the night. Healing falls like warm rain and our open, tired bodies receive the blessing of seeing in the dark that ritual brings.

So, dear traveller, welcome to the journey. Your Inner Shaman is waiting and we have some foundations to build. We will begin with *Awakening the Dancer,* learn about *the Nine Steps of Ritual,* work with *the Tree of Life,* meet the elemental powers and undertake *the Mesa Elemental Practice* before having our first encounter with the Inner Shaman. Then the doors between the worlds will be open.

Ready? Steady. Go…

CHAPTER 1

Movement Is the Medicine

'Consciousness is only possible through change;
change is only possible through movement.'

ALDOUS HUXLEY

In a shamanic context, 'medicine' means the uniquely creative and healing power and essence of being that is within us all. Discovering, claiming and making best use of your medicine is your Inner Shaman's *raison d'être*. Doing this involves the reclamation of your physical body, your emotions and your imagination. The potentiality of this relationship between your *terra firma*, your heart and the imaginative power of your soul is the basis of the shamanic practice I'm going to share with you now. A friendly relationship with your body will give you physical presence. It is also the key to accessing the kinaesthetic intelligence it holds – intelligence that has evolved over nearly 14 billion years. Once you are present in your body, you also gain access to the emotional intelligence of your heart. Together, they are the fertile land in which the ever-evolving story of your soul can evolve.

Your body holds all your memories. If you want to know how, Dr Bessel Van der Kolk has written an excellent book entitled *The Body Keeps the Score*. And if you want to understand the importance of releasing traumatic memories from your body, I cannot recommend it highly enough.

The Inner Shaman has two ways of working with this. The first is what is traditionally known as *soul retrieval*. This is the healing of past events that affect us strongly in the present. It involves bringing our present resources to past situations in order to transform our relationship with them and the meaning we have ascribed to them. Traditionally, this is a process that has been carried out by shamans working on behalf of their patients. In this book, I am going to show you, step by step, how to do that work safely and effectively for yourself.

The second is what I call *soul emergence*. Soul emergence is the natural developmental process of the unique blend of body, heart and mind that makes up your soul. In essence, it is the process through which you discover yourself and your purpose in this world. Through the chapters of this book, it is my intention to help you to get to know what your Inner Shaman already knows. This will help you to emerge more fully as who you are – empowered, responsible and able to harvest what you came into this world to create.

You don't need to go and buy a whole bunch of shamanic paraphernalia to begin. Your body, heart and mind, a little curiosity and a nugget of courage are all you need to go on a very deep shamanic journey. You already have the most powerful shamanic tool right inside you: the bright intelligence that is the dancer who lives in your muscles and bones. This intelligence is movement and rhythm itself. It is the rhythm of life, the very drumbeat of your heart.

From a shamanic perspective, the central wound of the industrial world is that we rely almost solely on the brilliant but limited intelligence of the mind. If the mind is disconnected from the innate wisdom of the body and the emotional intelligence of the heart, its undoubted virtuosity can lead us away from our own ground and disconnect us from the life under our own feet. And if we are disembodied, we don't experience life directly. Since religious creed made God into an unreachable, untouchable and dogmatic idea and turned the body into a vessel of sin that had to be subdued at all costs, we have imposed an idea of separateness on our body and heart and the physical world around us. It is easy to see how this world-view has landed us in our current situation. Whether that situation becomes an ever-escalating crisis or motivation for change remains to be seen.

I have a profound predilection for the ongoing evolution of our human species as part of the ongoing evolution of life itself. And I know that if we are to play a part in the future of life on Earth, quite simply we need to update our priorities and create a new story. And we need to do it fast.

What is the role of the Inner Shaman in this? The Inner Shaman stands at the doorway between the physical world of manifest reality and the imaginal world of what we dream. They can help us to create a new dream for ourselves, for our loved ones and for the community of life itself. The Inner Shaman knows that the intelligence of the body-heart-mind working together is the vessel through which divine intelligence in human form can evolve through us all. And the best way I know of engaging that possibility and committing ourselves to it is shamanic dance.

SHAMANIC DANCE

Shamanic dance doesn't mean learning somebody else's steps or following pre-formed patterns. It comes from our capacity to listen deeply and allow the power of life that is movement to move us, ground us and, when necessary, shake us to the core. It means remembering what we are made from and breaking the chains of self-consciousness and the outdated stories about who we are and who we are allowed to be. It means reclaiming the birthright of free movement and ecstatic states that the dancer in our bones remembers. That dancer has the quickest access I know to the Inner Shaman.

If dance isn't your thing, worry not. It wasn't mine either. However, over the past 30 years of practice and teaching, I've come to respect our natural ability to give our body and heart to the rhythm. We all have this ability. I've worked with people of all ages across a vast array of cultures and experiences, and though self-consciousness is inevitable at times, it really doesn't take much to quieten the mind and allow the intelligence that animates the body to show the way.

Gabrielle Roth, to whom I was apprenticed for 18 wild years from the age of 24 to 42, taught me that shamanism is indigenous to its own culture. What that means is that though we can learn a lot from shamans from other cultures, to make full use of whatever we learn, we have to translate it into the everyday language and experience of our own lives and culture. All shamanic practice is rooted in the healing journey that shamans must take for themselves. Once they know the terrain of their own healing through their direct experience, they can then lead others on that journey.

As we begin, it's important that we are standing on the solid ground of shared intention. So, to be clear, in this book I am not training you to lead others in the practices I will share with you. To hold space for others, you have to go through an intense series of initiations. My intention here is to introduce you to your Inner Shaman so that you can take your own healing journey deeper and use what the Inner Shaman brings you to bring your spirit and what you dream to this Earth in service of life.

Gabrielle taught shamanic practice through the body and through free movement. So do I. Movement Medicine is a fusion of everything Susannah and I learned from Gabrielle and everything we have learned from the many other shamans around the world we have been blessed to be apprenticed to and work with. It embraces neuroscience and contemporary understanding about how we can transform the past into wisdom in order to live more consciously in the present and create a future of which we can proud.

The edgy, catalytic artistry of the Shaman in you already knows that everything you encounter in life is nothing more than life's invitation to give your body to the beat until all that is left is the dance itself. Gabrielle taught me that the false split between body and spirit was causing the very greatest part of our suffering. Her teaching was a silky river of soulful poetry inciting the true self inside each of us to rebel, take back the territory of the body and the heart and then to dance to heaven and hell and back again, if we had to, to break through the fixed patterns of the ego and gain access to the unlimited imagination of the soul.

That was a revolution as shocking for me as being struck by lightning. I hated dancing, or at least I thought I did. Gabrielle taught me that what I actually hated was feeling self-conscious, awkward and disembodied. She taught me how to shift my attention from what I was thinking about to what was happening in my body and my heart. She taught me to give my body to the beat so that the dancer in me was awake and available to help me let go of absolutely *everything*. She loved the empty space that is the result of giving ourselves to the dance. She called it the *Silver Desert*, and I was astonished to discover that dance was the most direct method available to take me there too.

I danced with Gabrielle for the first time in a workshop in London in 1988. I was certain, with that extraordinary ability I had to make everything about me, that as I danced, people would stop to laugh at me or tell me I was in the wrong place, but nothing could have been further from the truth. Within 20 minutes, the dancer in me had been unleashed, and not only did I break out of my tight little box, I realized that the box was of my own making. Very soon, I'm going to show you, too, how to shift your attention from thinking about what's happening to embracing what's happening as the doorway into your own dance. Whatever you may think now, that will be possible for you. In all my years of teaching, I am yet to meet anyone who is unable to do this once they've made the choice to give it a go.

Before we begin, though, it may be helpful to recognize that a common challenge we face when beginning something new is our history with learning. I hear stories all the time from adults whose childhood was defined by an education system that encouraged them to be more like parrots than creative individuals. No offence to parrots intended. But 'good' students were those who could regurgitate what they'd been told on command. Making mistakes was frowned on. But the willingness to make mistakes is a prerequisite to learning, just as being uncomfortable is an inevitable aspect of stepping into unknown territory. And a little shamanic tinkering with the curriculum through the power of free movement would create more of what our world needs now – embodied, open-minded, emotionally intelligent adults who know they have something of value to give. After all, that is the only genuine road to fulfilment and contentment I know.

Shall we?

PRACTICE: AWAKENING THE DANCER

Since this practice is the foundation of everything else I will invite you to participate in, I've made two simple recordings to support you with it. The first includes my guidance and the second is an instrumental-only version. You can download them both for free at: www.darlingkhan.com/shaman

Timing

You will need a minimum of 15 minutes for this, but feel free to take longer.

Preparation

- Wear loose and comfortable clothes. Don't wear socks.

- Clear a small space in which you can move freely. You don't need much room. Many of our students have told us that they do this practice in the toilet cubicle at work when they need to reconnect to their body and heart and clear their mind before an important meeting or just to survive a difficult day!

🖉 Invoke the Unbroken intelligence of life that is animating your body, making your heart beat, your blood circulate and your cells replace themselves. That intelligence is the movement of life itself. It is the dance, and the way it moves through you is *your* dance. Visualize this intelligence running through your body, from the top of your head to your toes, and from your toes to the tips of your fingers. Imagine your whole body is free to move and to let go. Good. Let's begin.

Practice

🖉 If you have access to the recording I've made for you, just press 'play' and off you go. If not, find a piece of music that is repetitive, rhythmic and free from any distracting lyrics.

🖉 If beginning feels awkward, don't worry. I remember how I felt in that first workshop with Gabrielle. Self-consciousness may be present. It's in your head. So I'm going to ask you to forget what's In your head. Forget about doing a 'good' dance or the 'right' dance and focus on your feet, as far away from your head as you can get. Imagine that your feet have just been waiting for this opportunity to show you what they can do. Imagine they are a gift that you're really excited to discover. Breathe a little more deeply and let your feet begin to play with the rhythm. Then let your body follow. Remember, there is no right or wrong here. So simply give your feet to the beat and follow them. Forget about being fascinating and let yourself be fascinated. Keep going for a minute or two. Don't hold back, but do make clear that your intention is not to push your body further than it can go.

🖉 Great. Now keep your feet moving and shift your attention to your lower legs and knees. Mobilize your joints and let your knees lead. Really let them play. Your dance may not look like any dance you've ever seen. Good! Keep going. Feel the physical connection between your feet and your knees and follow the rhythm for a minute or two. It's absolutely fine to slow down or to speed up, but if your thinking ever takes over, move a little more quickly and refocus on your lower legs and knees. Repetition is good. Free movement is good too. You don't have to try to be creative. The dancer in you already is.

✍ Now expand your awareness to include your feet, knees, hips and pelvis. As you invite your hips to show you what they've got, feel free to welcome your sexual energy into the dance. Not for anyone else, simply because your sexual energy is a wonderful force of creativity and healing.

✍ And as you release your hips and let the rhythm move them, relax your jaw. Follow what comes and keep on moving. Energy naturally moves in waves. Follow it. Spend anything from 90 seconds to two minutes on each part of your body, but if you're engaged, feel free to go on for longer. If you get tired at any point, don't stop, just move more slowly until your energy picks up again. It will. Finding the breath that supports your movement is key. The more strongly you move, the more breath you need. Don't be afraid to make an effort. Some days, the dance and the breath come easily. Other days, you have to work your body back into movement. Don't think of this as a dance unless it helps. Keep inviting the dancer inside you to lead the way.

✍ This practice is teaching you the power of focusing your attention. And energy follows attention. So shift it now into your backbone, the very core of your body. Imagine that your backbone is listening to the rhythm and let it respond in movement. Pay attention to your lower back, middle back and upper back. Discover what your backbone can do. Turn, bend, twist gently.

✍ Connect your backbone, hips, legs and feet. Feel how your awareness is expanding as you focus on more and more of your body. Some parts may move more freely than others. Notice that, but don't push those that don't move as much.

✍ Give yourself permission to feel pleasure in your body. You are reclaiming your body and it's totally cool to enjoy it. Don't worry if other feelings arise too.

✍ Okay, expand your awareness to include your shoulders. Isolate them first as you bring your focused attention to them. Feel the sensations in them. Are they warm or cool? Free or stiff? Just notice how they feel and go on moving.

✍ Now let your shoulders lead. The dance is different when we allow different parts of our body to lead. Have you noticed that? The more freedom you give to the dancer, the more movement vocabulary you will discover. This translates into more potential creativity and freedom of expression on the dance floor called life.

✍ Your shoulders now invite your elbows into the dance. Elbows can be sharp. They can cut through space and define that space more clearly. Invite your elbows to lead now and let the rest of your body follow.

✍ Your elbows go on moving and invite your hands into the dance. Your hands are connected to your heart and to your emotional intelligence. Give them permission to welcome your heart into the dance. Welcome in how you feel right now. Let your hands lead. Go on breathing and play with tempo and opening your body and closing it. Both are good. Feel how your hands and feet are connected through your body. Let them be partners in the dance for a while.

✍ Well done. So far, so good. Any time you feel self-conscious or self-critical, just come back to the simplicity of what you're doing and make the choice to be more fascinated by the sensations in your body, your breath and the rhythm. As you gain more and more ground in the dance, you can let go more. Try opening your body and expanding into the space. Try the opposite too: close down your body and focus on what's happening inside. Say yes to the dancer in you. Say it out loud. Go on, give yourself some encouragement.

✍ Okay, now that your whole body is moving to the rhythm, you can include your head. Invite your head to move with your backbone, as if it's just an extension of it. Be gentle with it. Let it move, but don't throw it around. Move slowly. Then more quickly. Expand. Contract. Learn new movement vocabulary.

> It's quite common when you give your body and heart permission to speak that they will. If emotion comes, treat it like weather. We need the rain to water the deserts inside us. We need the sunshine. We need the dark of the night. Whatever arises, notice it and give it to the dancer inside you. You can say it loud: 'Dear dancer, please show me how this experience moves.' You are free to move with it. You are free.

> You may lose concentration. This is natural. When you do, smile to yourself and bring your attention back to a place in your body where you can feel energy. Let that part lead. And from there, reconnect to your whole body and follow where the dancer leads. Slow is good. Fast is good. Small is good. Big is good. Just follow for a while. It's a wonderful liberation to sense that there is an intelligence in your body that can lead when you let it. Sometimes, your body may need to shake. Sometimes sound comes. This is all completely fine. It's not necessary to understand what's happening with your mind. Simply be present and let the dancer in you embrace it.

> It's likely that some parts of your body will be more accessible to you than others. At this stage, just be aware of this. You don't need to do anything about it. Later on, as you gain confidence in the intelligence of life that is movement, you will be able to go more deeply into those areas and the Inner Shaman will help you take back full ownership of your own land.

> Keep going with this for a minimum of five minutes, but feel free to go on for longer if the dancer has more to show you right now.

> When it's time to close, slow your movement down. Come to a still place. Let gravity take the weight of your body, feelings and thoughts. Spend some time just standing or sitting still, feeling the

life inside you. Thank your body and thank the dancer in you for showing you a little of what they've got.

🖎 Once you feel you have come to the end of the experience, drink a glass of water and then make a few notes about the essence of what has happened.

Congratulations. You have awakened the dancer in you. Well done! Really well done!

I never get bored of this practice. I've done it thousands of times, but every time is different. Whenever I begin a ritual, I start here. The intelligence of the dancer within is the ground for all that follows. You will discover this for yourself as we continue.

❦❦❦❦

As we end this first chapter, I want to acknowledge that life is unpredictable and change seems to be the only constant. It is often a sudden and unexpected change that lights the spark of transformation in us. Somebody dies. We get sick. We lose a job. A relationship breaks down. Pain in life is inevitable. How we dance with it isn't. The dancer within is as free and spacious as the Wind, as powerful and transforming as Fire, as grounded and stable as Earth, and as deep and mutable as Water. So let's move on. Now that you've met the dancer, let's turn our attention to setting up ritual space.

CHAPTER 2

Ritual and the Imaginal Realm

'A ritual is the enactment of a myth. And since myth is a projection of the depth wisdom of the psyche, by participating in a ritual, you are being put in accord with what is inherent within you anyhow. Your consciousness is being re-minded of the wisdom of your own life.'

JOSEPH CAMPBELL

The shaman dances with one foot in the everyday world and the other firmly planted in what the 20th-century French scholar and mystic Henry Corbin termed 'the imaginal realm'. The imaginal realm is very important to the shaman. Through his study of Persian and Sufi texts, Corbin discovered that this realm was believed to be a field beyond physical consciousness, a field that, though related to our imagination, existed independently of it.

Imagination is a powerful force that all shamans need to learn to use. Everything that has ever been created began as a dream or an idea – something imagined. And through imagination, we can connect to the imaginal world. My imagination is within me. The imaginal exists beyond me. There's a difference between, say, imagining my great-great grandfather standing behind me and calling my great-great grandfather's spirit to stand behind me and share his wisdom with me. Whether I pay any attention to him or not in the imaginal realm, my great-great grandfather's spirit has an existence independent of me.

As we go further on our journey with the Inner Shaman, I am going to invite you to explore the unlimited power of your imagination. At the same time, I'm going to encourage you to root your consciousness in your physical body as much as possible. On my own journey, I've found that being focused and present in my body, heart and mind has been and continues to be the best way to open the door to and receive guidance from the imaginal realm.

THE WAKING DREAM OF RITUAL SPACE

The Inner Shaman's number one method for accessing the imaginal realm is through what is sometimes called *the waking dream* of ritual space. Ritual space is a space of refuge and recharge for the Inner Shaman. And yet I meet many people on my travels who think of ritual as anything from a whole crock of mumbo jumbo to a downright dangerous pastime that will get you into trouble of all kinds. Such is the victory of organized religion and a certain rigid style of empirical thought that for many, ritual has become something to avoid and even be afraid of. Shamanism too. The story that shamanism is dangerous is at the root of the fear so many people feel when confronted with it. So before I invite you to enter into ritual space, it's important to consider where this fear has come from.

For the shamanic traditions of the world, the powerful blend of state and Church became deadly with the witch hunts that began in Europe in the 13th century. Powerful propaganda backed up by fear and violence claimed that the old traditions were evil, dangerous and ultimately a route to eternal damnation.

Now, it's true that there are and always have been some dodgy shamanic practitioners out there who have no moral issue with abusing their power for personal gain or, worse, to do harm. But dodgy practitioners are not unique to shamanism. They are to be found in every profession, often as a result of the fragility of the human ego. Knowledge of shamanism and shamanic ritual, like any power, can be used to harm or to heal. It's down to us.

But back in medieval times, there was real danger in following the old ways. New stories were proclaimed from the pulpit and found their way into the human psyche. Sex was for procreation only, and the body and all of its 'unholy' desires needed to be controlled. Revelry that celebrated the turning of the seasons was outlawed, the Earth became dark and the once magnificent Pan became the Devil. Cavorting with the spirits of nature was a sin. Heaven was far away and accessible only to those who kept the rules. A priest was needed as an intermediary with the divine. Sunday was the day to pray and rewards were to be had only after we had died, and then only if we had done as we were told.

The terrors of 700 years of Inquisition meant that any natural and independent connection to the divine had to be hidden. Parents had to teach their children to hide any difference from the perceived norm lest it be taken as a sign of some unholy association with some out-of-control force. I consider this massive disempowerment of human beings to be one of the greatest con tricks of all time.

Worse, once this marriage of state and clergy had taken centre stage in Europe, it went on tour, 'civilizing' the rest of the 'uneducated world'. Numerous genocides followed as the colonizers inflicted their own version of 'divine love' on anyone and everyone who happened to get in their way. In the world-view in which the most powerful story must dominate all other stories, the shamanic traditions of indigenous peoples didn't stand a chance.

And then came science, and the whole shamanic story was relegated to the fantastical, the 'weird', the exotic and the marginalized. If it couldn't be measured, it didn't exist.

Having acknowledged this historical backdrop, let's bear in mind that for much of human history, ritual was as everyday as making a cup of tea in the morning. Connecting with the powers of nature to pray for a good harvest probably felt as necessary to our ancestors as going shopping does to us.

BALANCE AND RESPONSIBILITY

When I began working with ritual, the blend of the history of shamanism and having grown up in a culture where the rational was king meant that I had difficulty quietening my mind. I had to train myself to focus. And over time, I had to take my own healing journey with the stories that arose in me as I deepened my practice. As we go deeper, I am going to share the tools that I have found most effective in not just healing the past but transforming it into medicine.

Contemporary shamanism is not about going backwards to regain some illusory original shamanic paradise. It's about integration of what we now know. It's about learning that where we place our attention is the main factor in how we experience life. It's about building a bridge between the rational and the mysterious, between the known and the unknown. I know how often I've had to reassure my rational mind that I have every intention of continuing to respect it as a good friend and ally in learning how to put what I learn in ritual into practice in my day-to-day life. Strengthening the bridge between the imaginal world of ritual and the rational world of the everyday, is of vital importance so that we can travel safely and consciously between them. Making peace between them has been one of the most challenging and rewarding aspects of my own journey as a shaman in the modern world.

For anyone working with shamanism in the modern world, there is a need to balance the imaginal realm with what we call reality. Too much *reality* according to the rational mind can create too fixed a point of view. Too much of the *imaginal realm* can lead to one of the major shadows of shamanic practice – the disembodied, disempowered running away from reality that is often rooted in the fear that we will fail to bring our dreams into this world. I suffered from this for many years. Consequently, the shamanism I practised earlier in my life was more of an escape from the world than a harnessing of the inspiration I received in the imaginal realm. My own journey has partly been about coming into my body and heart, learning how to use my mind and accessing the power I need to bring my dreams to Earth.

The shaman knows that to make a difference in this world, they must gather and use power. If you choose to take this road, it is your responsibility, shaman or not, to ensure that there are people in your life who both support you on your journey and who are not afraid to challenge you. Whatever role we play in life, the more powerful we become, the more important it is to consciously and continuously dedicate the power we develop in service of life in a way that makes sense to the very soul of who we are. Any shaman or person of power who is not consistently doing this work is likely to fall prey to the temptations of power. A central part of my own training has been focused on recognizing the need for ongoing and fierce self-inspection, including in ritual space. And the stronger I become, the more vital is the honest mirroring of people further down the road than I am.

A few months ago, on my 55th birthday, I lit a ceremonial fire on our land and sat by it to drum and pray. It was a beautiful evening – bright, with a strong breeze blowing from the South West. I drummed and sang to call all my spirits and to call to the spirits of the trees, the river, the fire and the strong granite earth of Dartmoor beneath my feet. I was deep in the meditation, and in my inner world I was seeing beautiful spirits all around me. After a while, I heard the quiet voice of the Wise Elder inside me. It simply said, 'Ya'Acov, open your eyes. Everything you see in your imagination is right here. Go on, open your eyes.'

And so I did. I couldn't believe the simple magnificence of the landscape I was in. The trees around me were dancing with the wind. The flames of the fire were dancing too. The stream just behind me was singing its springtime song. My heart was wide open and I felt delightfully defenceless. I stood up and started to dance and to say the prayers of gratitude that were apparently just waiting for me to voice them. The more present I was, the more I felt connected to both the physical landscape around me and the spirits of nature. The imaginal world was right there in front of me and I realized, with a wry smile, that with my eyes closed, I was shut off in the closed loop of my own imagination. With my eyes open, I felt a potent mixture of utter vulnerability and spiritual strength. And the more I played, sang and revealed my heart, the more those spirits and my own personal allies revealed themselves to me.

This recognition of the difference between being safely cocooned in the closed loop of my own imagination and revealing myself as I am to life was the first teaching of my 56th year. And in the months that have followed, I have noticed a subtle but telling difference in the level of connection I feel to both the imaginal realm and the physical world around me.

The ceremonies I hold today are designed as healing spaces in which participants get to value their creativity and to recognize the power they have to create with whatever hand of cards life has dealt them. In ritual, we can safely remember that a wild, raw, untameable dreamer is a part of who and what we are. A good shamanic ritual is a strong container in which we can remember what supports us, rebalance the light and the dark inside us and see things as they truly are. We can lift our awareness from the grindstone and see our lives from a wider perspective.

In order to support you in entering into ritual space, I have developed a nine-step process that maps how I construct, enter into and integrate the experience of ritual in a safe and rewarding way. These nine steps are good for all the rituals I will share with you in this book. Let's go through them together and make a stronger connection between the imaginal world of the spirits and the physical world we are here to create in.

🌿 PRACTICE: THE NINE STEPS OF RITUAL 🌿

Timing

You will need a minimum of 15 minutes for this, but feel free to take longer.

Preparation and practice

I am going to describe each step in general and then invite you to do it.

1.   Setting your intention

The intention for your ritual is the direction your inner compass is pointing in. The clearer the intention, the clearer the space. Intention is not a rigid thing, but since the mystery that ritual invites us to explore is so vast, focusing on one or two things at a time is helpful. When we visit our family in the Amazon, Manari tells the people we bring with us that staying with that focus is of great importance so that we don't get distracted by all the things that come into view as we enter the imaginal realms.

Now set your intention for this ritual: to learn about the nine steps of ritual and to strengthen your ability to connect the physical and the imaginal.

2.   Physical preparation

Preparing yourself by taking a shower, wearing comfortable clothing and preparing some food for afterwards makes the entrance into ritual and the re-entry into everyday life smoother, while slowly and quietly preparing the space you are working in by beautifying it, setting up a small altar (see *below*) and preparing any music you may need gives your psyche the time to recognize that you are about to enter ritual space. (I will talk more about music in a later chapter.)

42

It is also important to tell any people who share the space you will be working in that you are preparing for ritual and to negotiate needs (yours and theirs) before you begin.

3. Invocation

Invocation is the bridge between the everyday world and the imaginal world. It means calling your allies into your awareness and your space. Over time, your relationship with the universal allies such as the elements will deepen if you give them your attention. And as you work more with the Inner Shaman, you will discover your personal allies, or what a shaman calls their spirits. For now, your invocation will focus on calling the elements into the four directions around you and sensing those elements inside you. I will talk more about getting to know your allies, both universal and personal, as we continue our journey.

✍ Standing at the centre of your space, turn to the South and, by paying attention to the physical earth that your body is made from, call your awareness of Earth as an independent elemental power and ask this element to be in the South of your circle, for instance: 'I call the power of the Earth from the South. Please come and show me how to connect the Earth of my body with the body of the Earth so that I can learn to stand up on solid ground.' In the same way, in the East, call Fire, in the West, Water, and in the North, Wind. (If you already have experience of working with the elements in different directions, this is not a problem. In reality, all elements are in all directions.)

✍ It helps to have a simple physical representation of each element that you can place in the four directions. This can be as simple as a piece of paper with the word written on it or as complex as something you have made to honour that element.

✍ I was taught that dedicating your work right at the outset by saying the words 'For all my relations' out loud makes the wider context clear to you. Why not say them now?

4. Acknowledging your condition

In order to work effectively, acknowledging the simple truth of your condition as you begin is vital. Ritual is not an escape from reality but a deepening of our relationship to it. Once we honestly acknowledge where we are, our capacity to be creative with it is restored.

✍ I suggest that you do the *Awakening the Dancer* practice again (p.29) with the clear intention of getting a deeper sense of your condition and inviting the dancer to find the shape and expression of how you are right now. Include anything that has arisen for you in reading and working with this chapter. Acknowledging what is true makes more space for the heart, and this is always good for ritual.

5. The focus

Your *Awakening the Dancer* practice will bring you into the here and now, focus your attention and open the door to the imaginal realm where you can do your work and receive guidance.

✍ Without expectation, turn your attention to each direction and each element, one by one. Staying in movement, invite the element within you to show you how it moves. Have a simple dialogue, introducing yourself and offering any gratitude you can (this is mightily important). Be open to any guidance that comes from each element as you open yourself to it.

The five elements

6. Bringing back the gifts

This stage of ritual is to do with recognizing what you have received and naming it. Ritual space is very much akin to dreaming. And just as when we wake from a dream, it's easy to forget the details of what we receive. I always have a notebook with me in ritual. Writing notes or drawing images or symbols that represent the gift of the ritual in physical form is all part of this stage.

 ✍ So go ahead now and make a few notes in a journal fit for purpose.

7. Integration

This is the work of paying attention to how we are going to plant the seeds of the ritual into the garden of our life. It's a time for clear thought and mindful enquiry into what changes we may need to make so that the gifts of the ritual can grow.

✎ Take some time to think about how paying attention to these elemental powers may be helpful to you in your day-to-day life. How can you deepen your awareness of them and your relationship to them? Think of one simple action you can take in the days to come that will help you to know that you are integrating this ritual, for instance thanking the Waters of life when taking a shower, thanking Fire when you cook or thanking the Breath of life when you take your first breath in the morning.

8. Closing the space

Just as we invoked our allies at the beginning, it is important to release them at the end.

✎ Thank and release the allies you called. It takes some time to get used to speaking out loud to spirits that you can't usually see, but your voice is an important tool.

9. First steps

The final part of any ritual takes place over the hours and days that follow. It is to consciously take the small steps that help you to know that you are planting the seeds from your ritual. The only difference between a vision that remains in the imaginal world and one that becomes an everyday reality is the action you take.

⚜ ⚜ ⚜ ⚜

Since practice makes the master, I suggest you practise these nine steps often, so that they become natural to you. You are gathering the tools and preparing the ground to meet the Inner Shaman. With their help, over time you will develop the art and structure of ritual that work best for you.

Before we continue, a word to the wise: the Inner Shaman knows when they need help and will avail themselves of it whenever necessary. On my own journey, I have often had the need for external human support, whether in the form of a good therapist, a mentor or a practitioner of the healing arts. This is not a sign of weakness – quite the contrary. Transcendence happens from time to time and it's a wonderful blessing. But it doesn't replace the need to own your history and transform your relationship to it. Modern therapy and trauma work can help and are complementary to shamanic work. If at any time you find that the practices I invite you to explore bring up material that is difficult to handle by yourself, please get the help you need.

In the next chapter, we will work with a really helpful practice that I have found is universal to shamanism. Let's take a deep breath and dive in.

CHAPTER 3

The Tree of Life and the Three Worlds

*'All theory, dear friend, is grey, but the
golden tree of life springs evergreen.'*

GOETHE

The Tree of Life is the most universal of shamanic symbols. On a physical level, we all know that trees are of massive importance to our planet's ability to sustain life. The life cycle of a tree is also rich with potent symbology that can help us to connect with the teachings of nature.

Imagine an acorn. Perfectly formed. Fresh, green and bursting with life and potential. Imagine a handful of acorns. None of them are the same. Let's find a good place to plant them all. Some open, fertile ground, not too wet, not too dry, with plenty of light, where the lie of the land gives some protection from the wind. Let's put our little acorn friends in the ground here. Good.

Now let's watch the scene through the bright lens of our imagination as the seasons pass. We see those husks breaking under the ground as the force of life, moved by some invisible will to be itself, expands beyond its previous form. Something inside each unique acorn compels it to do its best to fulfil its potential and become an oak tree. And so it shatters its previous form and risks opening itself to the elements around it. It begins a powerful dance with the nurturing Earth and the Fire of the warming sun and the cleansing Waters and the clear Air that, as wind, teaches it to dance. It's a wonderful thing to see an oak sapling moving with the world around it and, season by season, following the complex pattern of its own DNA as it puts down its roots and reaches for the sky.

Ten years go by, then 20, then 100. The tree follows its own internal development and at the same time is shaped by everything around it. The mature tree is a blend of what it is and what it has come into contact with. Envisage yourself walking around the mature oaks, touching them, leaning into them. Go on, give one of them a hug. No one's watching. Isn't every one of them majestic? See how big those roots are, how wide that canopy. What a complex dialogue these oaks are weaving with the dark earth that holds them steady. What a channel they are creating through their strong trunk and the chaos of their branches as they hold their leaves out to the vast light of the sky.

Imagine it's winter and one of those great trees is dreaming. Fall into its roots with me and feel how the intelligence that began life inside an acorn has matured into a tree and is already dreaming of spring. But for now, lean into the nourishment of winter. The blessing of no growth. Of resting in the dark. Then feel the change as time moves through the seasons. Each spring, there is a surge of life – wild and free in youth and sweet and sensually slow in older age, but always willing to expand beyond current form in summer. Each autumn, there is a glorious sharing of colour, a falling back, a superb surrender. As one more cycle of life passes, one more circle of experience and self-knowledge is tattooed around the solid, secret core. A branch falls; another grows, filled with the tiny buds of tomorrow's forest. As the years go by, the tree is shaped by storms and droughts and snow and sunlight. It provides shelter for a huge number of beings. Trees display such generosity towards one another and towards life. They show us how to receive everything we need and give everything back in return. They go about their business, taking long, even breaths, in and out, slow but silently rhythmic. As time goes on, they decay and die, as all living things must. But all the experience that they held nourishes the earth that brought them forth.

The Inner Shaman learns from the power and intelligence of the natural world around them. For our friends in the Amazon, the forest is everything. It is their grocery, their pharmacy, their clothes store, their building materials supplier – everything. Going beyond that, they understand its importance for all life everywhere. All the indigenous shamans I know have shared with me how the wisdom and love of the Great Mystery is directly available to anyone who pays attention to the intelligence of nature. In the Amazon, the kapok tree, which towers above the forest's canopy, is considered sacred, a gateway to the spiritual realms.

Working with the Tree of Life as a shamanic practice helps in both the physical and the imaginal world. Physically, sensing roots going down from our own two feet gives us a much deeper experience of being grounded. Being aware of the core of our body – the trunk – can help us to stand up straighter inside ourselves, and flexibility in our backbone creates more fluidity in our heart and our feelings, while 'opening our branches' to the wide open space above us can create a sense of more space and blue sky thinking in a busy day. The following story from one of our apprentices illustrates how embodying the symbol of the Tree of Life helped her. (I will share the practice she mentions with you later in this chapter.)

> At one point, we were practising the Tree of Life meditation. I had danced the Tree of Life so many times before, but in this moment of dance my relation to the tree changed. Rather than simply visualizing the tree, I realized in my body that I AM the Tree of Life. More than that, I felt how this had been true for my whole life. Up until that moment, I had never really stretched out and inhabited my roots and outer branches. I felt so strong and centred and I felt: 'I am stable and I am nourished by the Earth and now I really can stretch into the sky and the sun to grow and expand.'
>
> After that, I did the Tree of Life practice every morning, not because I 'should', but from an inner call to feel this connected in my life. This practice helped me to be much more stable and grounded in challenging situations, especially in my work. I understood my work in a new way. I saw that I am called in when other people or organizations have lost their roots, or do not have the inner strength or orientation to stretch out to the sky and see the bigger picture. The more I embodied this, the more people around me felt it, and it has been a big help in all areas of my life.
>
> MARTINA WERTHMANN, CONSULTANT

THE THREE WORLDS

The roots, trunk and branches of the Tree of Life represent what shamans around the globe call the three worlds – the roots represent the Lower World, the trunk the Middle World and the branches the Upper World. What are these worlds?

The Middle World

The Middle World is the world of our everyday experience. It is the place of physical reality and, for a shaman, the place where what we dream, either consciously or unconsciously, comes into being. It is the manifest reality of our everyday life, the direct result of what rises from the roots of the Lower World and what descends from the branches of the Upper World. The Middle World is our trunk, heart and guts – the place where we experience life. The beat of our heart is like the beat of the shaman's drum, illuminating deeper truths and dispelling the fog of our daily affairs to reveal ourselves and the world more clearly. With each year, a shaman's heart and knowledge of themselves widen and so can include and accept more fragments of soul, more broken shards, more mysterious and Unbroken jewels, and more possibilities of expression as the Self matures in its unique expression.

In my experience, when visions and ideas rise from the depths or fall from the sky and land in the Middle World, they are usually pristine in nature and without an instruction manual. Bringing our highest inspirations, aspirations and dreams into the unpredictable physical reality of the Middle World takes courage. It involves becoming aware of our own unconscious and recognizing what Susannah calls not just our blind spots but our blind domains. It involves the willingness to let our inspiration evolve and develop, and usually it involves a lot of work! But I can tell you this: working towards a dream that has meaning for you is very different from working without meaning or a satisfying purpose.

The Lower World

Naturally, the health of any tree is hugely affected by the health of its roots. In amongst the roots of the Tree of Life rests the deep potential of that which is usually out of sight – the unconscious. All our experience bubbles away here in this underground cauldron. Tragedies and delights, victories and defeats become the hidden motivations that drive the story of who we are and the actions that arise from that story.

Travelling to the Lower World gives us the possibility of discovering the roots of any situation in which we find ourselves and seeing what has been hidden in the dark. The Lower World is also traditionally where we connect with an important aspect of a shaman's support system: power animals. Power animals are spirit allies. They are usually animals with whom we have an affinity or who carry qualities that we need to develop in order to be who we are. When travelling in the Lower World, I was always taught to ask any animals I came across if they were showing up to help me at that particular moment or if they were offering a more long-term relationship. It took me some time to discover my more long-term helpers and to recognize what was needed from me to maintain those relationships in a good way.

The Upper World

The Upper World is where we go for an overview. Following the drum, we open to the sky, to a place where we can unfurl the wings of our imagination, catch the wind and let our mind soar. We learn to listen to the very fine guides made of light who live here and help us to see the big picture. The Inner Shaman knows how important it is for us to lift our eyes from time to time. We can get so caught up in the details of our life that we forget what actually matters to us. The Upper World is the place where we can see the connections between the choices we have made and the experience we are having now. We see what we are doing with the cards we have been dealt. We remember the contexts that make up the multiple fragments of our identity. We see our people and their experiences. We see how often our unhealed past is acting itself out to create an equally traumatic present.

WISDOM FROM THE WORLDS

A shaman will often have a relationship with a particular tree somewhere in nature that acts as their centre-point or *axis mundi*. They will visit it often and make offerings there so that they can work with this place in the imaginal world without physically having to be there. In my work with the Tree of Life, I access this place through the repetitive rhythm of drum and body moving together. This focuses and opens my awareness so that I can travel through my body into the imaginal realm of the Lower and Upper Worlds and bring back what I discover there to help myself in the Middle World.

With every important question in life, a shaman leans in to hear the whispered wisdom of their ancestors and the yet-to-be-formed dreams of their descendants. They know that we are all only holding this torch of life for a while before passing it to those who will follow. In the Upper World, we can receive the guidance and gain the perspective that can help us to see our mistakes and the consequences of them. And, perhaps more importantly, we can see that the road ahead is as yet unoccupied by consequences. Whatever we see on that future road is at most probability. Change how we are and how we act now and we change the probability of the outcome.

My first experience of travelling into the three worlds happened in a ritual I did for myself not long after our son was born. I felt in need of guidance in this new chapter of my life and so I set up my space with the intention of seeking out that guidance. I danced and drummed until my mind was quiet enough to focus and the road opened to the imaginal world. My body went into a repetitive movement and I entered the Lower World through a door in the roots of the Tree of Life. I found myself in a workshop with some small men in overalls. I watched as they took my body apart, cleaned me up and put me back together again. They then threw me up into the sky, where I was surrounded by ethereal wraith-like spirits who communicated through light. I asked them the question that was the focus of my ritual. Their answer was simple but life-changing: what I did was much less important than how I did it. Receiving this guidance was so helpful at that time when I felt under pressure to succeed and support my family.

As I have developed my own way of working with this ancient medicine, I have come to connect more and more with the Tree of Life that I see every time I enter into ritual. The more I get to feel that tree within the roots, trunk and branches of my own body, the more I can connect to it. When I am holding ritual spaces for others, we always have something to represent the tree at the centre of the room. The more present each dancer becomes in their own body, the more energy there is in the centre, and through that, everyone is free to make their connection with the Mystery in their own way.

🌿 PRACTICE: THE TREE OF LIFE 🌿

The intention of this practice is to explore the three worlds of the Tree of Life and to get a deeper sense of where you are in your life through that exploration.

Timing

You will need a minimum of 15 minutes for this, but feel free to take longer.

Preparation

🖎 Set up your ritual space and prepare yourself. Ideally, find a beautiful, strong tree somewhere in nature where you feel safe and private. Introduce yourself to the tree, share the intention of this ritual with it and make an offering – a pinch of tobacco, a piece of fruit or a piece of chocolate will suffice. It is the *feeling* in your offering that matters most. If it's not possible for you to do this in nature, don't worry, you can do it in your own home – the imaginal world is always accessible to us, so imagine a beautiful, healthy, mature tree right there in front of you.

🖎 As before, do your invocation by standing at the centre of your space, turning to the directions and asking the elements to be there: Earth in the South, Fire in the East, Water in the West and Wind in the North.

🖎 Place a simple physical representation of each element in the relevant direction.

🖎 You may wish to add: 'I am calling to any and all help and guidance from the Lower and Upper Worlds that is here for my highest good and for the highest good of all I love and care for.'

Practice

✍ If you have a drum, feel free to use it. If not, put on some shamanic drumming music. The instrumental version of the downloadable track from the first chapter will be fine (p.29).

✍ Go through the *Awakening the Dancer* practice again (p.29), acknowledging your condition and bringing yourself into movement. Make sure you are as present as possible in your body, aware of your emotional condition and as focused in your mind as you can be. As always, don't overdo it and don't hold back.

✍ Keeping your body in motion, feel into the roots, trunk and branches of the Tree of Life inside you. Strong feet and legs connect you to the roots and the Lower World. A flexible and strong trunk keeps you connected through your heart to the Middle World and everyday life around you. Consciously and carefully, stretch up towards the sky and feel the branches connecting you to the Upper World and the wide-open space and light it is made from.

✍ Still moving, see the Tree of Life in front of you, either in your own imagination or represented by a physical tree. Imagine a door opening up in the roots and imagine yourself walking in and down a spiral staircase, lit by beautiful lanterns all the way down. Go on down into the roots. Pay attention to what you notice in the roots and in the space around you. When you reach the bottom of the stairway, step through another door into a wide-open plain. See what you see and call out to any animal helpers who can support you in your life at this time. If nothing comes, don't worry. Sometimes it takes a while. If an animal comes, find a way of communicating with them. Ask them if there is anything in your unconscious that it would be helpful to become conscious of at this time. See what comes. It doesn't matter if you don't understand it immediately. Sometimes understanding takes a while.

✍ Ask this Lower World guide if they are here just for now or are one of your long-term allies. Thank them and ask them if there is anything further you can do to thank them and to strengthen your connection with them.

   🖎 When you've finished your conversation, come back up the stairway, and when you get back to the Middle World, keep on climbing.

   🖎 Making sure that your physical body is still moving, imagine the stairway spiralling up through the trunk of the tree into the highest branches. Notice the different quality up here as you find a pathway into the Upper World. Look around and call out for your guide in the Upper World to reveal themselves. Again, if nothing comes immediately, be patient. Ask again. Guidance can take many forms. It may come as a feeling in your body, as words that you hear, or as a visual image. Don't leave your body, but expand your awareness to include this space. Your body's rhythm and movement will anchor you, so your imagination can open.

   🖎 From this vantage point, look down on the road your life has taken. See your origins and the whole journey of your life up until now. Witness this with a sense of love and acceptance and truth. Your guide can help with that. At the same time, be honest with yourself. There may be hurt, anger or grief down there. Just notice it for now.

   🖎 Ask the power of the Upper World to illuminate the road you are on, where you have come from and where you are headed. Give your attention to the road ahead. What do you sense about it? What do you want from it? How do you imagine it, not from a place of fear but from the broad perspective of the Upper World?

   🖎 When you feel ready, come back down the same way you went up.

   🖎 Your body is still moving to the rhythm. Open your eyes and confirm: 'I am here, at the centre of my circle, rooted, connected and present.'

   🖎 Thank the Tree of Life in whatever way feels appropriate.

   🖎 Make a few notes about your experience.

- ✐ Think of one simple action you can take in the days to come that will help you to know that you are integrating this ritual.

- ✐ Thank and release your allies.

Well done. Take a little time to congratulate yourself.

※ ※ ※ ※

With practice, your work with the Tree of Life will enhance and broaden your perspective. It will also help you to strengthen the connections between your unconscious, conscious and superconscious mind. Working with the Tree of Life inside you as a dance will undoubtedly support your grounding, your standing tall and your presence.

Each step we take together is preparing the ground for you to meet your Inner Shaman. In the next chapter, we will continue by working with the elemental powers of Earth, Fire, Water and Wind.

CHAPTER 4

The Unbroken and Your Elemental Nature

*'Nature is not our enemy, to be raped and conquered.
Nature is ourselves, to be cherished and explored.'*

TERENCE MCKENNA

Let's come back to the concept of the Unbroken that I talked about in the introduction. The Unbroken is the intelligence of life that has been in constant evolution since this whole shebang got started nearly 14 billion years ago. A connection to it is vital to shamans the world over. And if you wish to evolve into the very best version of yourself you can be in this life, then I believe that a connection to it is vital to you too.

I want to invite you to take an imaginal journey with me so I can share with you where I first had a direct experience of this force. Imagine that we're in an old canoe carved from a large tree, travelling down a wide river close to the border of Peru in the Ecuadorian Amazon. New sounds, smells and sights awaken your senses and you have the spirit of adventure in your heart. Imagine the steady and warm presence of our indigenous hosts sitting up front guiding and at the back steering us through the deep fast-flowing waters of the Bobonanza river. The sun is setting and the sounds of the forest are changing with the fading light as we approach the bank of the river. The engine cuts out and the sweet thud of wood into soft earth tells us that we have arrived. It's the home of a powerful Achuar elder called Sumpa. I love this place. It is one of the most biodiverse environments left on the planet and one of my favourite places in the world. I am always deeply touched by the people and the power of nature I meet here.

Come on, I'd like you to meet Sumpa and his family. We step out of the canoe onto warm, brown earth, then climb steps carved into the steep bank and enter a sizeable clearing. In it stands a large oval house with a thatched roof and open sides. Inside, the warm glow of a fire and a family sitting round it emphasize the feeling of welcome. Sumpa, wearing a woven skirt, beautiful black and red seedpod beads and a yellow, black and red-feathered circular head-dress, stands to greet us. His face is painted in the patterns and symbols of his people.

He tells us he is glad we have come and that his tribe's elders have passed on stories foretelling the times we live in. He tells us that they have assured him that the rainforest will stand, despite the pressures to exploit and destroy it. They have foretold that this will happen through making alliances with different peoples from around the world. He looks at each one of us in turn and his warmth and strength touch us.

Imagine you start to hear the sound of a soft leaf rattle. And then the deep pulse of a drum. Overhead, the stars are dancing. A quarter moon has risen.

It was a night just like this when I first experienced the Unbroken. I had been working in ceremony through the darkest part of the night. It was still dark, save for the misty light of the moon and stars. The song of the forest just before the morning star heralds the arrival of dawn is exquisite. As I listened to that song, I decided to take a little tobacco to help ground myself after the work of the ceremony. Tobacco in the forest is different from the tobacco to which so many of us in the western world are addicted. It's pure leaf, with nothing added, and for the people of the forest, it's a master plant medicine.

I take some tobacco juice through my nose now and settle in to concentrate. I feel the weight of my body and the support of the dark brown earth and I feel myself letting go. My eyes are closed. Step by step, I deepen my breath, expand and include more of what is inside me and around me.

I feel a little pressure in my chest and then, like a rather stiff door opening, my heart widens and I feel flooded by the love of the plant, the surroundings and the melody of the night. Inside my body and my own circle, I am quietly ecstatic, calm and focused. My vision clears and my mind opens. I sense people resting around me, my wife close by. Our hosts have not yet stirred for their morning tea. I feel such love for them.

I open to the forest around me and I feel part of it. I sense the late-night hunters and the prey. I feel the trees breathing and the insects busy playing their part in this intelligent system. I feel it inside me and all around me. Everything is just itself. Nothing is trying to be anything other than itself. There is a peace in this that I've never experienced before. It's not quiet. Animals and plants are living and dying all around me, but nothing is interrupting the magnificent symphony of life. It's unfolding according to its nature.

As I fall deeper and deeper into my own place in this system, I see spirits on the other side of the river. They appear to me as the warrior shaman protector spirits I have met before. They are magnificent – fierce and uncensored. I hear their song and I am singing with them. We are singing a song I have never heard before, and though the language is not one I know, the words are a blend of sounds that make perfect sense to me:

We are the Unbroken.
We come to remind you
That in everything that lives,
We are there at the centre.

We are the harmony and the melody of the Wind, the Fire, the Waters
*   and the Earth combined.*
We have many names
And we are everywhere that life is.

We are inside you.
We are the roots.
We are the sky.
We are all around.

We are the ground
From which all healing grows.
We are the Unbroken and we come
To remind you.

Carry me with you.
I am the Unbroken inside you.
I am the Unbroken inside everyone.
I am the medicine that heals.

I am deeply touched by their presence and by the message I am hearing. I feel the sweetness and strength of the song in my foundations. I have never felt so held. The direct experience of being in touch with this 'Unbrokenness' outside me *and* inside me is a step further than I have gone before. I am meeting an essential state, and one that I sense has already changed a fundamental story inside me that has identified strongly with what is broken in me and in my fellow human beings.

Like so many of us, I have lived with a deep sense of what is wrong with me, what needs healing, what needs adjusting and fixing. What needs improving. I have worked hard to heal, and I don't regret that. Perhaps this is the harvest: the recognition that deep inside me, and all of us, there is the perfect intelligence of life evolving, just waiting to be recognized. I ask the spirits about this and they tell me:

The Unbroken is at the centre of life. It is there inside everything that lives. Knowing it does not heal that which is broken. It gives us the ground to heal from. It is the memory of that which remains whole throughout all experience. It is the intelligence that is the movement of the tides, the cycle of the seasons, the elliptical dance of the planets. It is the beat of the heart and the beat of the drum. It is the song you hear in nature. It is the pure medicine you are made from – the elemental building blocks of life that are always connected to the source. It is the source of life itself as it lives in you.

I felt that jaguar-in-the-body, butterfly-in-the-heart fusion that has become such a living metaphor for the blend of strength and sensitivity that is the ground of my work.

Maybe one day you'll join me on a journey to meet Sumpa and his family. For now, let's come back to what we so love to call the 'real world'. We've work to do and things to discover.

The best way I've found to stay connected to the Unbroken in the 'real world' is through my ongoing relationship with the elements. These aren't just signposts in the four directions; born from the *prima materia* of the universe, they are the fundamental building blocks of life. Our physical body is made from them. We are Solar-powered beings made of Earth and Water and our spirit is embodied and animated through the Breath of life. We all have the possibility of making an embodied connection to the elements and, through that, to a greater power and to the essence of the Unbroken.

Through the Earth of your body, for example, you can connect to the extraordinary intelligence and power of the Earth beneath you and experience what being grounded truly means. Through the spark of life inside you, you can connect to Fire, and through that to the power of the sun and the light of the universe from which the sun was born. Through the Waters, you can discover the shapeshifter inside you as you follow the cycle of water from an ocean evaporating into vapour, becoming cloud and rain, becoming a river and then finding its way back to the ocean. Through embodying the breath, you can experience the power of the Wind lifting you up and taking you past the boundaries of your mind into the wide-open space of the sky.

There is a fifth element, too. Though it's normally called ether, I prefer to call it Love. By that I mean that it's the universal force of attraction that keeps the planets turning at just the right distance from one another for the miracle of life on Earth to happen. It contains all the elements and is the essence from which they all came into being.

The elements are an endless source of teaching, creative inspiration and energy. Nevertheless, the shaman knows that relationship isn't a one-way street in which we are empty-handed, always asking for more. Reciprocity is a universal principle of shamanic practice. It describes the equal importance of giving and receiving and is the key to the kind of dynamically balanced and mutually enhancing relationships I believe we are all hungry for.

By now, you won't be surprised to read that giving your body to the dancer and asking that part of you to show you how the elements move is the best way I've discovered of embodying them. What I love so much about the process of moving with the elements is that because we are physically made from them, we don't have to rely on our imagination alone but can simply focus on the part of us that is each element and then invite the dancer to work with the movement and creativity that is part of its nature.

Before we do so, there's one more practice that I'm certain will support you with that. As a child, I used to do a ritual every night as I crossed the bridge from waking to sleeping. I would expand from myself to others, to the community, to the imaginal world and to the source. At the edge of my imagination, like an oasis of sweet water in the deepest desert, I would find the question that has guided me my whole life. 'My rabbi tells me that God created all this. Wonderful. But what *is* God?' Asking this question blew my mind each and every night as I burst out of myself and fell back into the arms of the Great Mystery. In that place, I felt connected to a power of love that held me and all things in its embrace. There were no answers. But the question was without beginning or end, and the Mystery it opened me to was nectar for my soul.

Later in life, as I developed my shamanic practice, this experience returned to me and became the basis for my work. I learned that this natural capacity to expand beyond ourselves but stay connected to our own backbone was the basis of our ability to connect authentically with the physical and non-physical worlds around us. I have found it extremely helpful in building a connection between the elements as they exist within us and the greater power of the elements as they exist beyond us. The same is true of the Unbroken. If I can touch the experience of the Unbroken inside myself, I can connect to it outside myself. It is also true that if I can experience the Unbroken outside myself, as I did that night in the forest, bringing that experience into my body will support me in experiencing the Unbroken inside myself.

Interoception

The foundation of this ability lies in something called interoception. Interoception is a new word from the relatively new field of neuroscience. It refers to the capacity to pay attention to the interior sensations of the physical body *and to describe those sensations in words*. People who are skilled at interoception have much better self-care because they recognize what their body needs when it needs it. Low interoception generally leads to poor self-care.

Interoception is also the basis of our ability to accurately perceive others, to the extent that there is a strong correlation between people with low interoception and violent behaviour.

In terms of working with the elements, we are much more likely to be able to connect with them as allies when we can experience them through our body and then expand into them as a power and intelligence that is also beyond our body. As chance would have it, this is the precise focus for our next practice.

🌿 PRACTICE: THE MESA 🌿
ELEMENTAL PRACTICE

Mesa is the Spanish word for 'table' and in many South American shamanic traditions, it refers to the safe space in which the shaman does their work. In Movement Medicine, it also stands for the Movement Energetics of Spatial Awareness. *The Mesa Practice* is the means through which we connect our internal experience with what is around us. We do this through expanding and contracting our awareness from the ground of our body. So, while remaining connected to ourselves, we come into relationship with others, the environment, the imaginal world and the source of life.

I will invite you to work with the *Mesa Practice* first, then use what this teaches you to experience your connection to the elemental powers within and beyond you, and through this, enhance your connection to the Unbroken.

Timing

You will need a minimum of 45 minutes for this practice.

Preparation

✎ Set up your ritual space and prepare yourself. As part of preparing your space, create a small altar in each direction that honours the element associated with it. This could be as simple as a bowl of water, a candle, a feather and a flower, but please feel free to give your creative energy and intention to this. It will be good preparation for the more complex rituals I will share with you later.

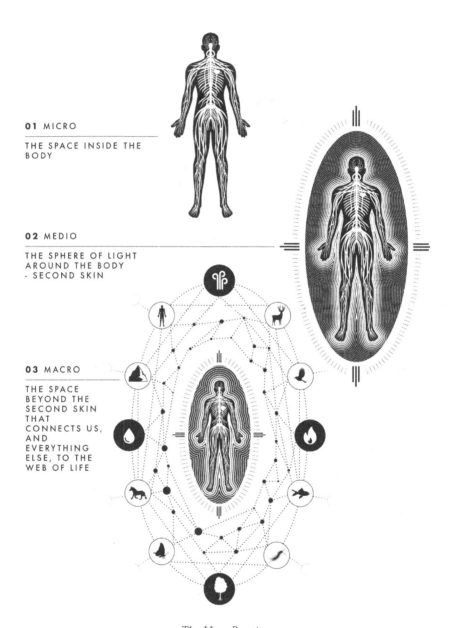

01 MICRO

THE SPACE INSIDE THE
BODY

02 MEDIO

THE SPHERE OF LIGHT
AROUND THE BODY
- SECOND SKIN

03 MACRO

THE SPACE
BEYOND THE
SECOND SKIN
THAT
CONNECTS US,
AND
EVERYTHING
ELSE, TO THE
WEB OF LIFE

The Mesa Practice

☘ As before, do your invocation by standing at the centre of your space, turning to the directions and asking the elements to be there: Earth in the South, Fire in the East, Water in the West and Wind in the North.

☘ Place a simple physical representation of each element in the relevant direction.

☘ You may wish to add: 'I am calling to any and all help and guidance from the elemental powers for my highest good and for the highest good of all I love and care for.'

Practice

☘ Take time for *Awakening the Dancer* (p.29), and in so doing, focus your attention in your body, quieten your mind and make space for your heart.

The micro dance

☘ Once your body is warm and your joints mobilized, slow down and, whilst remaining in movement, bring your attention to the surface of your skin and to the universe of experience within your body. You can do this following a plan (for example, from head to feet) or by just sensing where there is energy in your body, beginning there and taking your attention around the rest of your body as you bring it into movement.

☘ Breathe a little more deeply. Close your eyes if you wish. Move inwards and find words to describe what is happening inside your body. Say them out loud as you move. They can be as simple or as poetic as you want, for example: 'I feel warmth in the soles of my feet' or 'My lower back feels fizzy and bright.' I suggest that you include 'Here I am, as I am' from time to time as a reminder to both accept what is and to bring it into movement. Your movement may be slow or fast, but keep your attention focused on your *internal experience*. We call this the *micro dance*. It will help you to be more

71

aware of the subtleties of your experience and to include them in your movement and therefore in the dance of life.

 𝒜 It is likely and normal that you will discover that some parts of your body feel more or less alive than others. Acknowledge this and keep moving. Keep in mind that your intention in this dance is to discover the ground of your body and reclaim any ground that has been temporarily lost due to past experience.

 𝒜 Though it will take time and effort to reclaim your whole body, everything you discover is potential medicine. So, get to know the language of your body. The deeper you go with this, the more you will discover the powerful healing medicine of interoception.

 𝒜 Well done. It's time now to expand your awareness and, without losing your interoception, focus your attention on the life of the space immediately around your body. We call this your *medio*.

The medio space

 𝒜 As you continue to move, use your body to occupy your own circle, not by puffing yourself up, but by being present in your own interoception and aware of the space around you. Imagine your energy field is like a luminous cocoon around you, pulsating with the life inside you and strengthened by your connection to the elements in the four directions around you. Focus on the elements one by one and feel how they give you more ground, more clarity and strength, more fluidity and space. Spend at least five minutes on this. I cannot over-emphasize how important and useful it is. It will help you to strengthen the bridge between your internal experience of life and your capacity to express yourself and accurately perceive other people. It will help you to feel safer and support you in taking back the territory of your body and your energy field if the effects of the past have annexed it from the present. It will also support you in strengthening your boundaries.

✎ Keep shifting your focus from inside yourself (*micro*) to the edge of this 'second skin' around you (*medio*) as you move. Keep naming what you feel inside your body. Finding the words for it is part of the skill of interoception.

The macro dance

✎ Now use your body to sculpt this sensation and give it a repetitive movement. Involve your whole body. Say the words that describe the feeling out loud.

✎ As the next step in building your connection to the four elements, embody your experience, and in so doing, communicate with the four directions around you. Introduce yourself, your condition and your intention as you face each direction. Your communication is being expressed through your body and it is rooted in the *micro*, engaged in the *medio* and connected with what is around you through what we call the *macro* dance.

The Mesa Practice

✎ Go for it. Fill your whole circle with this feeling and movement, find the breath that supports this, and practise connecting your internal experience with the world around you. Stay with this *Mesa Practice* of expanding and contracting through the *micro, medio* and *macro* for a few minutes.

✎ Next time you expand your awareness and your movement into the luminous energy field around you, open your eyes and let in the environment in which you are moving. Name what you see whilst staying connected to your energetic boundary and your interoception. Make it as simple as you can. The intention is to remain connected to the feeling inside, whilst maintaining a sense of boundary as you connect through your body to the environment around you.

If you lose the connection to your interoception at any time, simply begin again. Keep moving through the three spaces of: 1. interoception (*micro*); 2. your energy field (*medio*); and 3. your environment (*macro*). You are learning a new and important skill. When I do this practice, I feel so present and grounded, and the more I have done it, the better I have become at staying connected to my own ground as I enter into relationship with the world around me.

Now for the second part of our ritual. This involves focusing on all five elements one by one and feeling how they give you more ground, more clarity and strength, more fluidity and space, and more aliveness at your core.

- Start with the elements inside you (*micro*). Find the shape and movement of each element (*medio*) and through this, invoke the power of each element beyond you, i.e. from the Earth of your body, connect to the greater power of the body of the Earth under you.

- Engaging physically with this and sensing how your energy changes with each element will result in a deeper experience. At the same time, follow the waves of excitation (higher energy) and relaxation through your body as you expand and contract.

- Speak to the elements as you move. Don't just ask for what you need, but, in the spirit of reciprocity, offer your dance as an expression of gratitude for what each element brings you.

- Spend a minimum of five minutes with each element.

- Once you feel replete and nourished by your practice, thank and release each element.

- Make a few notes about your experience.

- Think of one simple action you can take in the days to come that will help you to know that you are integrating this ritual.

- Thank and release your allies.

Return to this practice as often as you can. I never get bored of it and, like any relationship, the more attention I give to each element, the deeper my relationship with it becomes. And once you've got used to *the Mesa Practice*, you can use it on the dance floor of life – as you walk to work, sit in a meeting or as you fall asleep at night.

❧❧❧❧

Congratulations. Your foundations are now in place and it is time to meet your Inner Shaman.

CHAPTER 5

The Hollow Bone

A Personal Encounter with an Ancient Friend

'Start by doing what's necessary; then do what's possible; and suddenly you are doing the impossible.'

ST FRANCIS OF ASSISI

In the modern world, as traditional community structures have fallen away, we have had to recreate our idea of community and create new ways of making learning communities. Part of that work has been breaking away from the concept of communities as places of rigid taboos and dogmatic suppression of our individual expression. Indeed, the whole culture of the individual may well be a fierce reaction to some of the more repressive ways of the communities of old.

Though much of a shaman's initiatory work traditionally takes place alone in nature, Susannah and I recognized early on that creating a new template for community was an important part of our work. Finding the people alongside whom we had felt safe enough to learn was and remains central to our own healing journey. As Susannah eloquently explained, 'Our intention is to create community without conformity and encourage individuality without separation.'

Shamanism, like everything else, is going through a process of evolution. I know that the shamanism I practise now is very different from when I began. The main change has come from the growing understanding that we are collectively heading for big trouble if we don't make some radical changes now. Many of the elders from the surviving indigenous traditions of the world have received similar messages at this time. They have seen that they need to send emissaries into our world to share what they know and remind us of some of the basics we have forgotten. The urgency and speed with which they have stepped forward are indicative of the level of danger we are in and, given the way that most mainstream cultures have treated their indigenous people, also extremely brave. But the indigenous people we know have recognized that the prophesized time that will require the coming together of the best of all worlds is now. The shamans know we must find a way to weave together the collective wisdom and ingenuity of all cultures in order to thrive in a new era. Meeting your Inner Shaman will help you to know yourself more and, therefore, to know what role you can play at this 'all hands on deck' time in our human story.

Susannah and I have been told by the shamans and spirits of the traditions with which we have worked that it is our task to translate what we have learned into healing modalities that can tend to the specific wounds of our own people. This has been the intention of our work and it is the intention behind this book.

ONGOING COMMITMENT

The shamanic path involves a series of initiations through which a shaman learns how to be themselves and discover and deepen their connections to the land, the spirits and the Great Mystery that animates it all. They have to know themselves so that they can become the clear channel known as *the hollow bone*. This is the channel through which they can receive the healing for themselves that they will eventually bring to their community.

Like all shamans, I have come through a very testing journey and I continue to challenge myself to learn. I have made many mistakes along the way and I have made it my business to learn from them. I've noticed two things recently. One is, the deeper I go, the more embarrassing the revelations of my own unconscious become. The second is that I can be kind with what I uncover to the point where the pain goes out of it and it even becomes funny at times. As I've grown older, I've become much more accepting of my limitations, and I've been fascinated to discover that the more accepting I've become, the faster I have grown.

The ongoing work of self-discovery, which is the focus of the next part of this book, is a prerequisite for anyone working with power. We all know very well that collectively we have not handled our power very gracefully. This is down to the level of our development as a species. In other words, abuse of power is a systemic issue. What that means is that anyone working with power – and we all do, even if that is by refusing to touch it – has ongoing work to do so that our collective story with power can evolve. I cannot emphasize enough how important the conscious dedication of the power we gather through our work is.

The 'bone' in the phrase 'hollow bone' refers to the channel through which the shaman brings in healing. So, looking after the hollow bone on the physical, emotional and spiritual levels is a vital part of the Inner Shaman's work. Taking care of our physical body and giving it ample time and space to express itself in all areas of the dance of life is important, while ongoing self-questioning clarifies and shapes the self. This commitment is the key ingredient in allowing the Inner Shaman to safely surrender to a higher power and become the healthy hollow space through which the mysteries of the Earth and the sky can communicate.

If you have done the practices so far, then congratulations. You have created fertile ground on which to meet your Inner Shaman in a more direct way. If you haven't done them yet, I strongly suggest you do. Shamanism isn't theoretical, it's practical. It's an embodied here and now experience of the reality of interconnectivity. When I began, I recognized how much of my education had been rooted in theory. I had learned to be disconnected from myself and therefore from the world around me. Only at night, when I dreamed, did I feel connected. The waking world was much more difficult territory for me until I found the experiential work of shamanism, which is designed to heal the story that we are fundamentally separate from one another and the world around us.

Whether we realize it or not, we are all part of one huge complex web of intelligence that thrives on its diversity. Most of us haven't yet woken up to the simple fact that every member of this family of life on Earth, human or non-human, is worthy of a place at this table. This doesn't mean we have to like or even agree with one another, though if we were able and willing to discover the unique thread of wisdom inside each of the different ways of viewing life, I believe we could transform into a benevolent presence on Earth. And if we wish to even survive here, we have to agree a new set of principles by which to live.

Shamans don't live in a Walt Disney *Fantasia* land. They visit the imaginal realms in order to bring back inspiration for the next step they and their communities can take now. Part of their role is to bring the voices of nature, the ancestors and the spirits into the conversation. When we don't give nature a voice in the decisions that affect our future, we shouldn't be surprised when nature needs to make itself heard.

It's time for us to evolve. I dream that our current crisis, including all the polarization and suffering in our world, is bringing us to a collective initiation into a new level of consciousness.

For this to happen, we must experience the difference between working with shamanism as a set of ideas and allowing ourselves to embody our own unique manifestation of the Shaman within. The Inner Shaman is a universal archetype, but when we call them, it will be with the intention that they will help us to know our own personal version of this energy so that we can bring it into our life in an appropriate way. If we do that, it will benefit us and everything to which we are connected. And the more this happens, the more of us there will be who are listening to the non-human voices and the non-physical wisdom that are important aspects of our guidance system. If that happens, if nature has a voice in the corridors of power and the decision-making structures of our human societies, I, and many others, have seen that we can turn this corner and evolve.

INVITING IN THE INNER SHAMAN

Since I know that the archetype of the Inner Shaman is alive and well and just waiting for us to invite them into our lives, I am sharing with you the steps that have helped me and many others to do this in a grounded and empowered way.

Traditionally, shamanism is taught through practice. The apprentice learns by watching their teacher's way of working and by spending time alone in their own practice. In this way, they learn under the guidance and protection of their teacher. Through ongoing personal work, they discover who they are and how to work with the specific spirits, guides and energies that are particular to them. When this happens within a lineage, it is not just the teacher that is behind the apprentice, but the collective wisdom and spiritual power of that lineage. The practices I am sharing with you that are rooted in Movement Medicine have a strong lineage behind them. I am about to invite you to make a connection with some of that lineage so you can connect even more strongly with your Inner Shaman.

My own experience has shown me that as a result of growing up in the industrial world, with its mixture of brilliance and banality, I have needed to mend the connection between the rational and liminal worlds. When I began my practice, those worlds often clashed. On the one hand there was the glorious recognition that the imaginal world I had always known was in fact real. On the other, there were still bills to pay. So I know that the Inner Shaman needs a foot in both the practicalities of the everyday world and the inspiration of the imaginal world. All the practices that you have done so far have been designed to build a strong bridge between them and they will be a solid foundation for you now.

The Inner Shaman is a natural and skilled part of who you are. They have been with you as potential for a very long time. It is now time to meet them consciously and uncover that potential.

❧ PRACTICE: LET'S MEET ❧ THE INNER SHAMAN

Your purpose in this ritual is to become present in movement, call to all your allies and connect to your condition, your intention and the dancer in you. From there, you are going to invoke and experience the hollow bone and the archetype of the Inner Shaman coming through you.

Timing

You will need a minimum of one hour for this, but feel free to take longer. I suggest doing it at night just before you go to bed.

Preparation

✐ Set up your space with care and attention. Making sure that you have rhythmic music is vital. Using the same simple drum track will suffice. Don't use any music with lyrics in a language you understand. You don't want distraction, just rhythm.

✐ Once you have done your invocation and called in your personal allies and helpers, take time for *Awakening the Dancer* (p.29), then work with *the Tree of Life* (p.57) and the elements, including *the Mesa Practice* (p.69), to connect the elements inside you with the power of the elements outside you. I want you to be standing at the centre of your own circle, strong and fluid, connected to the elements through the roots, trunk and branches of the Tree of Life, feeling the spirits of those elemental powers around you and the physical presence of the elements within you. This is all about embodied presence and being in the muscle and bone of your being.

Practice

✍ Now, state your specific intention for this practice. I suggest the following, but feel free to improvise:

> *I affirm that this is a safe space for me to do my work. I call all support and protection. I call the ancient archetype of the Inner Shaman to come through me now. I wish to meet this ancient friend, this archetypal energy, and experience my personal connection to it. I wish to know the support and good medicine it is connected to so that I can know myself more, be who I am and give more of what I've got.*

✍ When you call, what do you notice in your body? Be patient. This process can be fast or slow, and the most important thing is that you are present in your body as the Inner Shaman lands there.

✍ Go through your whole body again, feeling the difference the presence of this archetype makes. Do any feelings or images arise? Breathe, move, expand and contract and let this shamanic being show you how they dance.

✍ Great. Now face the four directions one at a time and bow, introducing yourself anew from this place within you. I find it's best to speak out loud, even though at first I often felt like a fool for speaking to something I couldn't see! You might say:

> *I am the Inner Shaman inside this human being. I am finding my ground through this body, heart and mind. I wish to deepen this human's connection to the four directions and to the elemental powers. I am here to open the doors between the worlds of dream and manifestation.*

✍ Let the Inner Shaman visualize, embody and deepen your communication with the spirits of Earth, Fire, Water and Wind. Let their presence support you in letting go and allowing these elements to move through the hollow bone.

✍ Keeping your body moving, send your attention down into your roots. Feel them spreading out under the ground and invite the Inner Shaman to show you how they connect to the Lower World. Spend some time with this.

✍ Invite the Inner Shaman to connect with your branches and show you how they connect to the Upper World. From this vantage point, acknowledge where you are and where you have come from. See the challenges you have faced and the potential medicine you are carrying. See where you are in your life now and where your road is leading. Whenever possible, let the Inner Shaman be moved by their connection to what they perceive. As Gabrielle Roth used to say, it's time to 'disappear in the dance'.

✍ Now come back to your heart, to the trunk of your body and to the Middle World, the here and now, the bridge between the superconscious and the unconscious mind. Be in your body, with the Inner Shaman's guardians present in the four directions and above and below you. Ask the Inner Shaman to show you what resources they have for connecting with the Middle World and for bringing your heart's desire into this world for yourself and for all you care for.

✍ Call on all your helpers, known and unknown, to support you with this. Helpers may be teachers that you know, animal spirits, ancestors or the elements themselves. Trust yourself and know that the world of spirits is no different than the physical world in as much as there are all kinds of beings in it with all kinds of intentions. Knowing that you can say a strong and clear 'No!' is a prerequisite to being able to say a clear 'Yes!' Maintaining a clear boundary is always good when encountering the unknown. Whenever I meet energy that is unknown to me, I always ask: 'Are you here for my highest good?' I've been taught that the spirits don't lie. If you don't get an answer, the Inner Shaman will know how to make it unequivocally clear that you are only interested in meeting and working with energy that is there for your highest good.

✍ Ask the Inner Shaman whatever you wish to ask them, for example, 'Dear Inner Shaman, how am I doing with this ritual? Is there anything you would do differently?' Don't be surprised if they have a sense of humour, or are feisty or mysterious. Try to be open to who they are and how they perceive the world.

✍ Before you finish, take some time to simply allow the Inner Shaman to go inside the rhythm and move. For a little while, just put yourself in their very capable hands (and body, heart and mind) and let go. Become that hollow bone and, as you keep moving, see where this takes you.

✍ Once you feel you have completed the practice and have had whatever conversation you are going to have for now, ask the Inner Shaman to come into your dreams and to tell you how you can deepen your connection with them. Ask them what they need from you to become your friend and ally in life. Tell them that you wish to get to know them better over the days, weeks, months and years ahead. Listen deeply through your body, heart and mind. Answers can come in many ways – words, images and/or feelings.

✍ Once you have finished, thank all the powers that you called and release them. Have a good shake.

✍ Thank and release each element.

✍ Thank and release your allies.

✍ Make a few notes about your experience.

✍ Think of one simple action you can take in the days to come that will help you to know that you are integrating this ritual.

Congratulations. You have met and started a relationship with the Inner Shaman.

Remember that relationship is always a two-way street. That's why when you are asking to come into contact with the elements and the powers of life, it is good to give something back. Consciously saying thank you through your dance is good. Even better is doing something in your day-to-day life to honour what you have been shown. Why not plant a tree or make a donation to the Pachamama Alliance or Survival International to honour the indigenous peoples who have kept the essence of shamanism alive? Reciprocity is the key to a good relationship. And it is an act of empowerment to recognize that you have something of value to offer as well as something of value to ask for.

❧❧❧❧

This brings us to the end of the first part of our journey together. You now have an excellent foundation for going deeper. Shall we?

PART II

~

EMPOWERMENT

A Basket Full of Medicine

*'Power can be taken, but not given. The process
of the taking is empowerment in itself.'*

GLORIA STEINEM

Now that you've met the Inner Shaman, it's time to put them to
work in service of your own awakening. We're going to align
body, heart and mind in order to hunt and gather the medicine the
Inner Shaman needs to make the strongest impact possible on your
day-to-day experience of life.

At the same time as being concerned with your own awakening, I'd
take a guess that your Inner Shaman knows there's no such thing
as genuine shamanic practice that begins and ends with the self. On
my own journey, I've been taught that my liberation won't come in
isolation from the world, but in physical relationship with it. I've
found that to be true, and it has become even more relevant now,
when our way of life is causing so much damage to the natural world
around us.

The most powerful and intimate force that we've been given for
relationship is our creative sexual energy. How we are with that energy
has a huge effect on our vitality. And the Inner Shaman's power is
rooted in their vitality. So we'll begin our hunt for medicine with
a look at the dance of the apparent opposites of yin, the receptive,

creative energy of the universe, and yang, the active, conceptive energy of the universe, and your relationship to your sexual energy. Learning to harness your sexual energy for your health, wellbeing and empowerment is potent medicine for your Inner Shaman. And seeing how that primary relationship plays itself out inside you is of great importance if you are to effectively use your capacity to create.

Over the years, I've come to appreciate more and more that it is this physically present relationship with life in the Middle World that is the harvest of my work in the Lower and Upper Worlds. To bring what we learn to life, we need to be emotionally awake, courageous and able to let go and celebrate. Therefore, I'm going to invite you to ask your Inner Shaman to show you the landscape of your heart and your emotions. For the Inner Shaman, emotion isn't something to be got rid of. It's super-honed animal intelligence that we can learn from. And we need to harness the full power of our heart if we are to heal and bring our gifts into this world.

We will then open the door to the roles and archetypes that play a big part in the shaman's world. We will specifically work with transforming the roles that keep a particularly vicious circle spinning. That transformation from vicious circle to what I call the 'medicine circle' will be helped by connecting with four archetypes that will give your Inner Shaman greater access to their power.

Finally in Part II, I'll share with you a simple yet powerful embodied alchemical process that will be the basis for working more actively with where you are in your life. Your Inner Shaman has the capability to do deep work on behalf of your evolving essential self. They will serve you well as you discover more of who you are.

The Shaman's world is full of everything you can imagine and more besides. That's why they need a basket full of medicine. So, dear seeker, it's time for us to move on and do some good old-fashioned hunting and gathering…

Ready?

Okay. Let's talk about sex…

CHAPTER 6

Tender and Wild

Sexual Energy and the Inner Shaman

*'Originally and naturally, sexual pleasure was the good,
the beautiful, the happy, that which united man with nature
in general. When sexual feelings and religious feelings
became separated from one another, that which is sexual
was forced to become the bad, the internal, the diabolical.'*

WILHELM REICH

When I was young, I learned about sex from my father's hidden porn collection. It was a terrible education. My expectations about who I was supposed to be, how I was supposed to perform and what I might expect from a partner were so unrealistic. It took me a long time to recognize that disembodied sexuality is just as damaging to our inner environment and relationships as our disembodied way of life is to our outer environment.

Our human story with sexuality is definitely evolving. But my goodness, we've had some very rigid and strange ideas to contend with along the way. We've tried the 'sex is a necessary but indecent mechanism for procreation' method and it hasn't turned out too well. Perhaps those interested in controlling the majority needed to invent the 'sex is bad' story because they recognized that controlling our sexuality was the same as controlling our power. But even in traditions claiming to be about liberation, the 'sex isn't spiritual' story has been massively overdone. Worse than that, abuse has been rife for so long in so many areas of society that up until recently we've normalized it and collectively colluded in hiding it. And we've wrapped the most precious gift we've been given in shame. The massive success of pornography on the internet seems to me like a big 'Fuck you!' to all that shame. But it's not a good place to learn about intimacy, the art of vulnerability or the divinely wild and tender freedom of soulful sexuality. And it's certainly not the place to find our power.

Sexual energy is one way of describing the very source of life. It's how our physicality is created and it's the essence of our own fertility. It's enlivening, nourishing and empowering. In order to evolve, I passionately believe that we need to learn to work with it, in connection with our heart, and we need to release old stories that shame us, imprison us and disconnect us from our own source. This will lead to an increase in human consciousness that will be reflected in the way we are and the ways we act, and I believe that change will be for the better.

Maybe it's because it's where my own studies began, but throughout my shamanic journey, sexuality has been at the core. I have learned so much over the years and my shamanic practice with sexual energy has brought me to a place where I have healed my sexual shame and given sexual energy its rightful place in the temple and playground of my body, heart and mind.

To begin with, like many of us, I had all kinds of hang-ups and stories to contend with. So the revelation that sexual energy was the divine nature of life itself moving through me rather than some awkward fumbling towards a disappointing conclusion took some digesting.

I was taught two basic sacred laws and told that as long as I respected them, I wouldn't go wrong:

1. The first law was that the innocence of our sexuality should always be protected. In other words, our sexuality is a natural, beautiful and divine part of our humanity.

2. The second was: 'No means no.' Sounds basic, but if we were taught from an early age that our 'No' would be heard, there would be far less suffering in our world.

The truth of those early teachings touched me to the core. Perhaps the most important thing I learned was that sexual energy was the most potent force we had access to and we could use it to heal the wounding that we all carry in this area. The Inner Shaman has it within them to work through whatever histories we have and allow the divine gift of our sexual energy to be the basis for health, happiness and creativity in all areas of our life. I have been privileged to witness so many people transforming their sexual histories and moving beyond the damage and limiting beliefs imposed on them at an early age. As we move forward, you will learn to do this too.

Over the years, the subtler ramifications of these simple laws have also brought Susannah and me to understand that feeling safe in our sexuality is the golden key to intimacy. And intimacy is the prerequisite for a sex life that improves year by year, so that now, after more than three decades, our sexual relationship is better than anything I'd ever imagined possible.

But sexual energy is not just about sex. It's about being in our body and being connected to life. It's about empowerment and it's about creativity. Part of the shamanic training I did in the Amazon required that I was celibate for several months. I remember one night I was so full of energy that I found it impossible to sleep. In the early hours, I went out into the forest behind where I was living and found a quiet place to sit and meditate. I felt as if I had been connected to a power source and that power was surging through me in waves of genuine pleasure. I wasn't thinking about sex; my body had just become a channel for this energy to move through. Meditating wasn't working, so I stood up to move. I was barefoot and the soft earth beneath my feet felt full of life. As I moved, I felt the energy of the Earth begin to rise through my legs. For the first time in my life, I felt as if my body were being moved by a greater force.

The warmth soon spread into my heart. I was completely sober, but I felt such a rush that I was momentarily worried that my water had somehow been spiked. I felt the trees and the night birds and the wind all inviting me to let go. I felt so held that I began to cry. At the same time, I felt so strong. I felt tender and wild and free. Waves of pleasure were moving through me and my body felt both held and stretched between the Earth and the night sky. I was shaking, laughing and crying all at the same time.

And then I knew this energy was divine. This energy was sacred. This energy was sexual energy and it was a force of healing. Old chains were slipping off me and I felt a wave of fury that I'd ever felt any shame about this divine gift. Emotions rolled through me like a storm and I was left delighted and amazed by what my body and heart had remembered.

It's remarkable to me how fresh that memory remains, and I will forever be grateful to all the teachers and teachings that opened that door for me.

The journey between then and now has been a long one. There has been a lot of healing along the way, not all of it pretty! But suffice to say, I've never looked back. I now know, through my own experience and through working with many people who have suffered sexual abuse, that with time, safety, care and courage, healing is possible. And if your heart is still beating, I know it's possible for you too.

In our practice at the end of this chapter, I'm going to invite you to take a step towards harnessing your sexual energy as the force of empowerment, creativity and healing it was designed to be. The Inner Shaman knows that we are here to create with life, not just to create new life. Sexual energy is body, heart and mind in unison with the force of creation itself. What could be more spiritual than that? And what could be more of an opening for the unfettered and unchained magnificence that we are capable of being and giving?

And yet we live in times when there is a pandemic of sexual abuse and wounding. This is such an indictment of our way of life, and I am in admiration of all those brave souls who have stood up and named abuse and wrongdoing. I asked one of our students who has worked with her sexuality over many years if I could share an extract with you from her graduation project about her own healing journey from sexual abuse. I hope that you find it as moving and inspiring as I do.

I have been raped twice in my life – once as a child, at five years old; once as a young woman, at 19 years old. In my Movement Medicine apprenticeship group, almost half of us had been abused, both men and women. This problem has appeared recently as a real social phenomenon. [We are] a society that has totally gone against its own integrity.

I want to honour the one within myself who has always held the torch, the one who has always danced in me, listening to the little flame in the hollow of my belly, continuously guiding me and inviting me to grow. I want to make visible the link that passes through the hollow of my belly and my wounds, this link that has risen in me through dance, between the Earth, me and the universe, a silent and immense bond that fills me and envelops me with love, passes through my sex, my heart and the peaceful lake of my mind. This bond that has guided me all my life has held within it an unspeakable secret. At the same time, I have known, despite no recognition of this in the world around me, that my sexuality is sacred, beyond the sanctity of any chapel. I have been so proud and so ashamed at the same time.

The only way I've found for my childhood injury to be welcomed and 'treated' by the adult world is by dancing. In order to heal, I've had to integrate the taboo secrets of my past with the powerful, vital and sacred energy of the dance. This complexity has been a struggle. It has made me cross deserts of loneliness and sadness, but also given me a reason to live. And it has finally taught me that sexual energy is beautiful, legitimate and essential to life and the healing process. I have learned to be proud to have preserved it so well. It is a light that I have carried, and that I have even been able to transmit, thanks to my experience. The world really needs it. So many women have told me that they have dreamed of being initiated into this art of mastering their sexual energy. For me now, there is no difference between dance, the free and inhabited movement of the

body and the art of sacred sexuality. Indeed, this is now the main core of
my transmission here on Earth.

ANNE ENA BERNARD,
MOVEMENT MEDICINE AND *LES NEUF SOUFFLES* TEACHER

Thank you, Anne Ena. We've made progress and, thankfully, abuse is now being spoken about. But the wounding in our sexuality is deep and complex, and we have a long way to go to bring healing and understanding to its underlying causes. We still tend to have the idea that opposites are designed to fight rather than to co-operate and enhance each other, even though the unique blend of yin and yang that we are is anything but black and white. Creation is imagination without limitation, and therefore the diversity in our sexuality simply mirrors the diversity in nature.

Our collective sexual history needs both extraordinary patience and care and a damn good airing if we are to tell a new story. And since the imbalance of opposites in our culture is also inside us, there is internal work to be done. Your Inner Shaman is directly connected to the qualities of yin and yang, and I know that they can help you discover the infinite variety, dynamic balance and movement between them. This dance is your creative sexual energy and learning to work with it will be hugely helpful in bringing the Inner Shaman's healing presence and resources into play in your life.

I am purposefully using the terms 'yin' and 'yang' rather than 'masculine' and 'feminine' because I don't have space in this book to write about our confusion around gender and role. I'll just say this: for the most part, what has been called 'masculine' has done its best to dominate and possess what has been called 'feminine', whilst simultaneously what has been called 'feminine' has done its best to undermine and disempower what has been called 'masculine'. It's been a long war and it has gone on inside us and between us. And there have been no victors, only casualties.

There's a story doing the rounds that is doing a lot of damage. It says that the problem is 'toxic masculinity' and the answer is to give the 'healthy feminine' a chance to lead us to the Promised Land. It's my experience that it's the relationship *between* them that's toxic, rather than one side being responsible for the whole war. And it's the dynamic relationship *between* opposites that transforms the confrontational stance of polarity into the creative process of alchemy that we need now. Blaming and shaming is an inevitable and painful part of the process as long-suppressed secrets are exposed to the light of day. But it is not the answer, and until we are able to own the hurt and emotion that drive it, healing will not happen.

In our modern world, doing is valued above being, fast is better than slow and more is given more status than less. It's this basic imbalance between yin and yang that is at the heart of so many of our modern-day problems. I think the Taoists have got this one down. They say that out of the original Tao (the Great Mystery), came the one (the Creator). From that came the two (yin and yang). And from the juice of that original rendezvous came everything else. In the Taoist story, yin and yang are co-arising and equal in importance, strength and value. They get it on and everything else follows.

Between the Taoist Creation story and the Judeo-Christian one that has dominated large parts of the world for a long time, there is a telling difference. In *The Garden of Eden: Fall from Grace* tale, Adam, who'd already had to donate one of his ribs to create Eve, was led off the righteous path by her, after she'd been seduced to reach for forbidden knowledge by a devious snake. Poor old Adam, poor old Eve, and big, bad snake. Not the best of starts. Roll the clock forwards a few thousand years, and it doesn't look good. *Either/or* and *us and them* dominate much of the human landscape.

The yin–yang symbol gives us a big clue: in the black, a little circle of white; in the white, a little circle of black. Take those away and you've got the black and white blame game of 'us against them' that is at the root of conflict. Add them back in and you've got the possibility of the genuine alchemy of opposites that is the root of movement and evolution. So that's exactly what we're going to ask your Inner Shaman for help with in our next ritual. I'm going to invite you to take a step towards knowing the sanctity and power of your own sexual energy. We're going to do that through an embodied exploration of the yin and the yang inside you and the dance between them. In this way, the Inner Shaman can help you to change the balance of power inside you. And from that place of owning your sovereign right to change the story that you have inherited and followed, you can acknowledge what is and move towards healing and empowerment.

❦ PRACTICE: SEXUAL ENERGY ❦ AND THE INNER SHAMAN

The intention of this ritual is to explore the dance of yin and yang and to light the Fire of the creative sexual energy that arises when they are both fully present in the power and creativity of their expression.

Timing

You will need a minimum of an hour for this, but feel free to take longer. I suggest doing it at night just before you go to bed so that you can allow the echo of your work to deepen as you rest and dream.

Preparation

✐ Prepare your space with as much care and attention as you can. Time preparing for a ritual like this is time well spent. Bringing beauty and elements of nature into your space matters to the Inner Shaman. Anything that honours and celebrates the power, tenderness and life-enhancing medicine of your creative sexual energy is a good thing, while honouring the yin and the yang in your space states your clear intention to honour them within yourself.

✐ If you have a drum or a rattle, have it ready to hand, as using it will allow you to follow the waves of energy as they rise and fall. If not, I would suggest finding three pieces of music without distracting verbal content to provide the soundscape. The first should evoke the receptive, tender power of yin; the second, the active, dynamic power of yang; and the third, the meeting of the two. For the third piece, I would find a track that rises and falls in tempo and energy. Contrary to the clichéd, mechanical, one-track drive towards an ultimately disappointing peak, healthy sexual energy naturally moves between yin and yang, and you want music that supports you in shifting seamlessly between the activation, excitement and rawness of the peaks and the relaxing warmth and sensual safety of the valleys. It may be that you find a safe place to do this ritual outside in nature, in which case the soundscape of where you are will more than suffice. But if you know that your history in this area is challenging, feeling safe is of paramount importance.

✐ I suggest you begin by calling the Inner Shaman to be present through *Awakening the Dancer* (p.29) before turning to the four directions and invoking the elements and all your guides and allies. Ritual is an amplifier of energy, so it's important to get into the practice of calling for support well before you actually need it. And, as always, your invocation is a chance to name and communicate the intention of your ritual.

Practice

✐ Once your body is warm and your joints are mobile, take a little time to acknowledge your condition. How do you feel now, at the beginning of this enquiry into how your Inner Shaman can work with your sexual energy?

✐ Okay, good. Let's turn our attention to the yin aspect of being. As a dancer, explore the qualities of receptivity, listening and relaxation. Receive the breath, the sensations in your body, your emotional and mental condition and, through the element of Earth, remind yourself that your body, feelings and thoughts are being held by the gift of gravity right now. Give your weight to the Earth through whatever part of your body is in contact with the ground. I suggest you do this through the *Mesa Practice* (p.69) so that you see how it is to receive yourself in the *micro* and *medio*, and your environment through the *macro*.

✐ Stay with your interoception, inviting the sensations in your body to lead your exploration as you move. At any time, feel free to explore the yin quality with any of the elemental powers. For instance, explore the yin quality of Fire that calls people to sit together and share stories from the heart.

✐ Now let's explore yang. In movement, explore the active, outgoing, expressive nature of the apparent opposite of yin. Again, work with *the Mesa Practice*, and again, stay with your interoception and let the dancer lead. Actively explore the elements in this yang dance. The more creative you allow the dancer to be, the more you will learn.

✐ Now take a deep breath and let the Inner Shaman welcome your creative sexual energy into the space between the yin and the yang. Many of us are used to eliciting sexual energy through fantasy, and this is absolutely fine. But I want you to know that there are other ways too, the most basic of which is to recognize that your whole body is a potential erogenous zone. Feeling safe in your body and recognizing it as beautiful, powerful and as wild and tender as nature itself will help.

🖉 So go ahead now, whatever your emotional or physical state, and warmly welcome the divine gift of your sexual energy into your dance. It may be very quiet and still, and that's perfectly fine. However it is to begin with, invite it to circulate through your body and strengthen your internal presence and the luminous sphere around you. Healthy energy naturally moves in waves, and your energy will move, but please be patient (yin). Less haste may result in a deeper experience. At the same time, feel free to express yourself (yang). You are looking for the life that is catalysed by the space between yin and yang, so follow the waves of excitation and relaxation through your body as you expand and contract. Feeling pleasure in your body is a good thing, but as usual, and maybe especially here, there's no need to push and no need to hold back. Enjoy the wildness when it's there, enjoy the tenderness, and enjoy everything in between. It's quite possible that you may become emotional as you work with your body and heart in this way. That's fine. Simply acknowledge what you feel and put it all into the dance. For the Inner Shaman, emotion = energy in motion.

🖉 At some points in the dance, I suggest you repeat your own version of these words a few times out loud:

> Here I am, as I am. I affirm that my sexual energy is a gift from the intelligent source of life. I affirm that this energy is powerful, healing and a natural, innocent and divine aspect of who I am. My sexual energy is the energy of creation.

🖉 Spend around 15 minutes on this exploration. And then, staying in movement, bring the attention of the Inner Shaman to the roots of the Tree of Life. Ask them to show you the roots of your relationship with your sexual energy that are held safely in the quiet darkness of the unconscious and the Lower World. This is a fact-finding journey rather than a 'clearing the past' journey, so just be interested in what you sense, hear and see. I have been blessed to work with people who are healing their own and their ancestral sexual histories and I can tell you that patience and kindness are the yin keys to this journey. At the same time, though, knowing your yang dance will give you the courage to stay present and strong as you witness what is there.

🖋 Well done. Really well done. This is brave work. And it is vital work for your physical, emotional and spiritual health. So, follow the rhythm of the drum or the music now up into the branches of the Tree of Life and the Upper World and spend some time getting an overview of your timeline with sexual energy. Witness your history and the history of your ancestors. Utilize the unbroken health and strength that is present to balance any wounding that you see.

🖋 Looking forward, what do you dare to dream for the healing of your sexual energy within you, in your relationships and in your creativity as a whole? The future is partly based on the choices we make in the present. It is not set in stone. Over time, your Inner Shaman will show you how to use the power of your sexual energy for healing and creativity of all kinds. For now, spend some time on this overview, and when you are ready, come back down into your heart and the Middle World.

🖋 Focusing on your backbone and pelvis, bring what you have learned into your body (yin) and let the dancer express what you have learned in movement (yang). Move between these two until you find a still point right in the centre of your heart.

🖋 Find a prayer in movement and words that acknowledges where you are now and your intention to move forward with this exploration over the days, weeks and months ahead. Find a way to give thanks for the divine essence of life that is your own unique and ever-changing blend of yin and yang and is the power of creation present within you as sexual energy. I suggest you adapt the phrases you spoke earlier to reflect your experience as it is now and ground what you have learned.

✐ Thank and release each element.

✐ Make a few notes about your experience.

✐ Finally, think of one simple action you can take in the days to come that will help you to know that you are integrating this ritual.

❧❧❧❧

Congratulations again. You have opened a doorway to energy that is second to none in terms of healing and transformational power. Working shamanically with this energy may well bring things from the past to the surface. So it's a good time for your Inner Shaman to show you what they know about the shaman's heart...

CHAPTER 7

The Animal Intelligence of the Shaman's Heart

'I never saw a wild thing sorry for itself.'

D.H. LAWRENCE

M y father died when he was just 56 years old. I'd not long turned 30, and back then, 56 seemed young, but nowhere near as young as it feels to me now, not long after turning 55. It occurred to me this year that if I were to die at the same age as him, I would just have the grace of one more spring. In addition to everything I received from my parents, not least the gift of life itself, my father's early death has been a constant motivation to live while I can. It's a simple equation. The older I get, the more precious life is, and the more it sinks in that there really is no time to waste.

Having said that, my father and I didn't get on whilst he was alive. We were as stubborn as each other. And whilst there's no doubt that he gave me, my sisters and my mother everything he could in the best way he could, the more I became myself, the more conflict there was between us. A difficult relationship with either or both parents as we grow up has quite an effect on our emotional world. Whatever we need to do to survive the challenges of incarnation and childhood lays down patterns deep inside us. The deeper our friendships and relationships go, the more these patterns get activated. And the more there is to lose, the more our survival instincts come into play. The good news is that as we learn to accept these survival modes as parts of ourselves, we are more likely to change them for the better.

There are two major keys to unlocking our heart and setting it free. The first is to learn how to move creatively with all the different weathers of the heart. I originally learned from Gabrielle that for the Inner Shaman, fear, anger and grief are energies we need to learn to work with in order to awaken our joy and compassion. The second key is a good relationship with something called *Benevolent Death.* In the shaman's world, Benevolent Death is a being from the imaginal world who can become one of our greatest teachers in life. As our consciousness expands, Benevolent Death can teach us how to shed old skins we have outgrown. *Learning how to die whilst we are still living* is the shamanic art of letting go, another universal aspect of shamanism. So, far from being morbid, a healthy relationship with death makes the unlikely miracle of life on Earth that much sweeter.

It is my experience that when someone close to us dies, our relationship goes on. After my father died, I started meeting him in dreams and ritual spaces. At first, it appeared to me that he was still going about his daily business as if he hadn't died and I had to tell him respectfully that he had. In dreams, I put my hand through his body to show him he no longer had a physical body. Over time, I watched him progress. He would often show up in ceremonies and once I saw him with wings, flying ecstatically in the upper realms. I was astonished. In life, he was an entrepreneur with not much time for things of the spirit.

I asked him, 'How did you get those?'

He replied, 'Do you think you're the only one doing the work round here?'

I laughed.

Though I trust my experience, I have to concede that the father I see in ceremony could simply be my own internal sense of him and have no external reality at all. But I am less interested in discussing what the 'ultimate truth' of this is and far more interested in how, with the Inner Shaman's help, we can allow these kinds of experiences to empower us, bring us more dignity and deepen our capacity to be who we are.

In a recent solo ceremony to celebrate my birthday, I saw my father sitting quietly waiting at the edge of my circle as I drummed. At one point, I turned to him and asked, 'Is there anything you need from me?'

He shook his head softly and smiled in a way I rarely remember him smiling in life.

'So why do you always show up in ceremony?' I continued.

His reply was totally unexpected. 'To offer help if you need it.'

My jaw dropped. *'Help?'*

'Yes, help.'

'How long have you been showing up before I thought to ask you if you needed anything?' I asked.

'Ten years.'

He laughed.

My heart cracked and my eyes became a river. I couldn't believe it. I had been so used to being the strong one since he died, supporting him, and now here he was offering me support in a way that our mutual destinies never allowed when he was alive. My tears were a triple-natured blend of joy (that my father was offering me help in my work), shock (that he'd been available to do that for a decade before I'd thought to ask) and childhood feelings that took the opportunity to be heard.

My tears opened my eyes and my heart so that I could see the pattern of my life's journey from above. Much like a Zen garden, there was a perfect placement of form that allowed me to recognize that the artist that had made up this dream was beyond my everyday sense of self. Stepping into that garden that represented the journey of my life, I found everything making perfect sense. All I could feel was gratitude.

The thought came to me like a soaring bird appearing out of the morning mists: *Recognize yourself as that artist.*

Clichéd as it may sound, at that moment I knew myself to be an embodied soul on an eternal journey through the Mystery, connected to other souls through many shared projects. With my father at my side and my heart open, I felt I could trust myself not just to be connected to power, but to consciously wield it. For someone who had spent so much time in the shadow lands of considering power to be a dangerous thing to be avoided at all costs, this was a great victory. I now knew how important it was to wield power in service of life, and that became my prayer.

As I prayed, I looked up and saw a choir of my ancestors singing beautiful Hebrew nigguns (spirit songs). A strong line of light appeared through the dark sky, connecting my heart to the heart of the Creator, and for the first time in a very long time, I felt deep joy and peace in being Jewish.

For decades, my relationship with my ethnicity had not been an easy one. But at that moment I was able to distinguish between the dogma of religion and the pure and specific connection to spirit that I was being reminded of. One more ex-communicated part of me had returned, and as I welcomed it back and ended that ceremony, I remember thinking to myself, *My goodness, this unfolding never stops, does it?!*

'No, it doesn't,' came the laughing reply, and who knows who spoke those words?

The shaman knows that only the immanence of death or the felt presence of love beyond self will move us sufficiently to mature from purely consuming life to serving life. I have learned again and again that righteously telling people how to live or telling them off for how they are living just closes them up further. This is especially true in cultures where children have grown up being told so much of the time that they and their impulses are wrong. This creates adults who are easily closed down into defensive-aggressive postures when they feel criticized. The fact remains that life on Earth is a free-will gig. We get to choose what we do with the cards life deals us.

If we are to choose wisely, there is no way round the heart. Love has the power to crack us open and change our view. In a world where genuine self-love, meaning a mixture of warm acceptance and clearly intentioned discipline, is a very rare state indeed, we have one mighty Gordian knot to untie to access the emotional intelligence of the heart. When the Inner Shaman sees a challenge like this, they call up their resources and step forward with joyful intent into ceremony.

The road to self-knowledge is a healing road. And there's only one person in the whole wild universe who can choose to walk that road for you. And that is you.

I'm not going to paint a pretty picture of the work of self-discovery. At times, you may wish you'd stayed comfortably numb. But the harvest of doing the work is to be at peace with yourself, and in my experience, the less energy that goes into fighting to be myself, the more energy there is to create the dreams I came here to create.

For the Inner Shaman, the heart is the gateway to vision. If it is full of self-doubt, self-criticism, undigested hurts and fearful expectations. It's like trying to see through a window that hasn't been cleaned for a very long time. But to imagine that you need to clear up your entire history before you can see clearly is equally unhelpful. What is needed is the courage to enter the world of emotion. I hope that your work with the elements has already shown you that to know them, you don't have to understand them, or to know where they all come from and why. You simply need to experience them and how they move through the hollow bone that is the Inner Shaman's natural state. The same is true of your emotions.

YOUR ANIMAL HEART

As we've already seen, the heart is the bridge between the Lower World of the unconscious and the Upper World of the superconscious. To receive a guiding vision that really inspires you to be who you can be in this world, you need to engage your heart both physically, in terms of getting aerobically active, and emotionally. A healthy baby will laugh, cry, express their fear and anger in a sweeping torrent of feeling and then move on. As we grow, we learn what is acceptable in our family home and our culture. So we learn to mask our feelings and censor the emotional intelligence of our heart. The patterns we learn then go on repeating themselves throughout our lives, with the unfortunate consequences that our capacity to communicate clearly is much diminished and we expend an enormous amount of energy simply denying what we feel.

The Inner Shaman can help us break free of these patterns. They aren't interested in living up to someone else's ideals and attempting to bypass the heart in order to present an idealized version of who they are. They know that it is the truth that eventually sets them free.

The Inner Shaman knows how to call on animal emotional intelligence to support human emotional intelligence. All mammals share the same basic emotions. We learned from Gabrielle Roth how to dance with our emotions, and then, through research and practice, developed what we had learned from her. There are four emotions that the Inner Shaman needs to engage with. Together, they lead to a fifth and form a five-chambered mandala that is the foundation for developing fluent, embodied, emotional expression:

The Movement Medicine heart mandala

- In the South, we have the chamber of awakening, which relates to fear.

- In the East, the chamber of integrity, which relates to anger.

- In the West, the chamber of surrender, which relates to sadness.

- In the North, the chamber of gratitude, which relates to joy.

- In the centre, the chamber of grace, which relates to compassion.

Compassion, meaning 'to feel with', is the result of allowing ourselves to know the emotions associated with the other four chambers of the heart. If we aren't okay with any of these four, our capacity for compassion will be greatly reduced.

It's important to acknowledge that we've probably all experienced emotion in negative ways. Too much fear leads to feeling disassociated, overwhelmed and panic-stricken. Unowned or irresponsible expression of anger often leads to violence. Too much identification with sadness can lead to feeling depressed and waterlogged. And I guess we all know the 'sugar on shit' do-gooding saccharine sweetness of someone doing their best to cheer people up but just irritating the hell out of everyone.

All of these negative expressions of emotion are massively present in our world and, I would guess, in each of us too. It's so important to recognize that they arise from a distorted or wounded relationship with emotion rather than being the result of emotion; for instance, anger is an appropriate response to the breaking of boundaries. It has recently been discovered that one of the best ways for those unfortunate enough to have been sexually abused to work effectively with that trauma is to learn to box. Apparently, the physical contact of hitting a pad or a gloved hand is a much more effective form of healing than expressing anger in words alone. Anger, like all emotions, is a force that we need to learn to use wisely. Our emotional wellbeing is really down to our day-to-day relationship with all these basic feelings, and I cannot stress enough how important this wellbeing is for our health in every sense.

The best way I know of keeping the flow of the heart clear is to get physical and allow the Inner Shaman to move their way through the chambers of the heart on a regular basis so that we can experience the simple equation I learned early on my journey from Batty Thunder Bear, one of my first teachers:

$$\text{Emotion} = \text{Energy in Motion}$$

Where there's energy, there's life.

I guess that by now you're sensing it must be time for another practice. And you're right. The intention of this one will be to give space to the animal instincts of your emotional intelligence and, through the power of your heart and all the other support to which you have access, create, renew and enhance your vision of who you truly are and who you can become. If you are new to this work, you may want to take this in bite-size pieces. Going at your own pace with this kind of thing usually gets you where you're going in good time.

 PRACTICE: YOUR ANIMAL HEART

Timing

You will need an hour for this practice.

Preparation

- Set up your space and invoke your support in the usual way: *Awakening the Dancer* (p.29), greeting yourself and your heart and acknowledging the reality of your emotional condition right now.

- Once you feel present in your body, you're going to oil the doors of your heart by giving it a good workout both physically and energetically. You'll be hunting the moving shapes of your feelings rather than putting yourself under pressure to feel the emotions themselves. The purpose is to let your Inner Shaman explore a wider range of physical vocabulary for each chamber of the heart. If there is real emotion that needs to move, it will flow down the channel that your physical body is creating, either now or when that emotion arises in your life. The aim is to make friends with these emotions and deepen your emotional intelligence.

✍ You will need some good rhythmic music without verbal content. A shamanic drumming track like Track 5 on my *Shaman's Song* CD (Hay House, 2018) will work well.

Practice

South: the chamber of awakening; the deer

✍ Once you are moving and present, turn your attention to *the chamber of awakening*. Recognize the part of your animal intelligence that knows itself as a prey animal. I like to work with the grounded sensitivity of the deer. So go ahead and invoke the spirit of the deer through your movement. You are light on your feet yet totally connected to the ground beneath you. You are curious and very alert. When something scares you, you stop and orientate yourself. If you sense danger, you run. If something has really frightened you, you find a safe space to shake off any excess adrenaline.

✍ Go through these movements in a cycle, using your embodied imagination:

~ Move lightly on your feet and explore the sensitivity that keeps you alert to your surroundings.

~ Imagine something startles you. Freeze. Breathe slowly and deeply as you orientate yourself towards the perceived danger.

~ Unfreeze.

~ Melt into movement and run for your life.

~ Find a safe place and shake your whole body from the inside out to release any excess adrenaline.

⚘ Repeat this as often as you feel you need to, but five minutes will be time enough.

⚘ Thank and release the deer.

East: the chamber of integrity; the jaguar

⚘ Invoke the hunter animal in you and ask the spirit of the jaguar to come through you and take you into *the chamber of integrity*. Feel the difference in your body. The jaguar is totally secure in their own circle. Sense the grounded, fiery power in your body and the ferocity of your intent when you are hungry. Feel your capacity to protect what needs protection. Explore the explosive power within you (as always, taking care of your physical body).

⚘ Find your roar. For a short time, let this animal power help you find the movement of anger. Don't feel pressure to *feel* anger, just let the jaguar's power show you the movements that could support the clear expression of anger, were it to be present. Find your 'No!' and find your 'Yes!' Again, five minutes should suffice.

⚘ Thank and release the jaguar.

West: the chamber of surrender; the salmon

⚘ Now invoke through your movement the Waters of life and a master of the Waters, the spirit of the salmon. Imagine yourself totally at home in the Waters, in your fluidity and in your depths. Let your body and joints become fluid.

⚘ Invoke *the chamber of surrender*. Salmon are extraordinary beings: they know how to go with the flow and they know how to use their full strength to swim against the current to return to the place of their birth. Invite the spirit of the salmon to show you how to go with the flow and how, when necessary, to find the fluid strength to move against it. Feel how these movements might give you the courage to follow the flow and release the dance of sorrow and grief. Let go, again without the slightest pressure to feel any specific emotion. Again, continue for five minutes.

🖉 Thank and release the salmon.

North: the chamber of gratitude; the kingfisher

🖉 Still in motion, call to the Wind and invoke the spirit of the kingfisher. Breathe deeply, open the wings of your imagination and feel what it's like to fly with your feet on the ground.

🖉 Invoke *the chamber of gratitude*. Imagine you are free to feel joy, again without any pressure to feel anything. If you were joyful, how might this shape your body and your experience? Play, make space for your breath to move joyfully through you (five minutes).

🖉 Thank and release the kingfisher.

Centre: the chamber of grace

🖉 Now ask all these animal helpers to stay close by as you, as Inner Shaman, enter into the central chamber of your heart, *the chamber of grace*. Feel your roots going deep down into the ground. Feel the space you have created in your trunk and the strength and fluidity of your heart.

🖉 Reach up through your imagination into your branches and look down on your life. See it as your medicine path, your initiatory journey. Imagine that you can witness any aspect or situation from your past from a place of deep compassion and grace.

🖉 Find a simple way to acknowledge or bless the road you have travelled. Let yourself sense how your life has made you who you are, and if you can, open your heart to the possibility that your journey is a huge creative project.

✍ Now take a look at the road ahead. See it as the time life is giving you to both be and become who you are. Somewhere along that road, Benevolent Death is waiting. As I mentioned, Benevolent Death is a great teacher and a good friend. In my experience, it usually asks some pretty poignant questions like: 'If you knew you only had one more year to live, is there anything in your life you'd change?'

✍ Dialogue with Death for a while and then ask yourself: 'If I were to find the courage to let myself be and become who I truly am, who would I be? Who would I become? What is mine to give?'

✍ Continue to move your body and ask the deep emotional intelligence of your heart to help you feel and to experience a little more of your essential self. That vision can come through words, images or feelings. It can be a more yin process, which means that it feels as if you are receiving the answers from a greater intelligence than your day-to-day self, or a more yang process, which means that you choose to create in alignment with the inner library of wisdom to which the Inner Shaman has access. A blend of both usually works best.

✍ Trust your heart to receive what you are ready to receive. Try to find that mixture of kindness and discipline with yourself that is part of the shaman's wisdom. Whatever ingredients life has given you, the Inner Shaman is there to put them all in the cauldron and cook them down into the sweet medicine of self-knowledge.

✍ The answers to questions like those that Benevolent Death may ask you can take a while to come into focus. They may arrive in dreams or just as you wake up. The important thing is to be as present as possible for what comes. And be patient. Dialogue with Death again and again if you need to. Be clear that you wish to discover more about the mystery of who you are and who you can become in this world.

🖉 Finally, thank and release each element.

🖉 Make a few notes about your experience.

🖉 As usual, think of one simple action you can take in the days to come that will help you to know that you are integrating this ritual and commit to it.

❧❧❧❧

Congratulations are due once again. But this is just the start. With all of these practices, repetition will give you confidence and make you stronger. A blend of patience and passion helps, and your Inner Shaman has plentiful access to both.

CHAPTER **8**

Vicious Circles and Medicine Circles

The Importance of Roles and Archetypes

*'Shamanic healing is a journey. It involves
stepping out of our habitual roles, our conventional
scripts, and improvising a dancing path.'*

GABRIELLE ROTH

Vicious circles are self-perpetuating blame and counter-blame patterns which spiral deeper and deeper into negativity and destruction. They can happen within us and between us, and they frequently do. Our world is full of them and our media is full of the resulting aggravation.

Medicine circles are the complete opposite. They are rooted in positive stories and 'win-win' feedback loops that nourish and empower everyone involved. They are also self-perpetuating, but they create connection and hope, rather than destroying them.

Both circles begin with stories. Stories are the lens through which we perceive both ourselves and the world around us. Perceptions create feelings, and feelings motivate actions, and actions create outcomes that always reinforce the story we are telling. Shamans know that perceptions, like nature, are not fixed. And shamans are powerful people. If powerful people don't dedicate themselves to questioning their perceptions, problems will never be far away. The more powerful the person, the bigger the impact of those problems. This goes for the Inner Shaman too. In order to learn to trust the power of the Inner Shaman, fierce, honest and kind self-enquiry is required on an ongoing basis.

A responsible shaman will do their best not to mistake their perception of reality for reality itself. As a healer, a shaman comes to understand that when our pain body (the shapes, patterns and undigested experience from past difficulties and trauma that live in the physicality of the body) is activated, we see the present through the lens of the past. When that happens, we imagine that what we hear is what is actually being said. When human beings are triggered, they go into whatever pattern they have learned in order to protect themselves, and humans are masters of the self-fulfilling prophecy. This time-devouring theatre of suffering is caused by not questioning our assumptions about who we are, who others are and what life is. It's time for a change, and I want to show you how the Inner Shaman can help you to break out of some of the more common roles we play in these vicious circles and step out of the past into the present.

Here's an example. Many of my ancestors were murdered in the holocaust and my great-grandparents were refugees. I have inherited much of great value from them and I have also inherited expectations about life that may or may not be true in the present. One is the story that *I am an innocent victim*. When I'm in that story, I perceive myself as *morally righteous but powerless* and I perceive the world *as full of aggressive people out to get me*. This leads to feeling *afraid and in danger*. The action that arises from this is *to defend myself in any way I can*. The more powerless I feel, the more passive my aggression will be. This leads to *defending myself aggressively,* which creates the expected outcome that *people attack me*. In turn, this 'proves' that my story is true. Since in this story my focus is on what is being done *to* me, I don't notice my own aggression and so it seems to me that the obvious truth of the situation is once again that *I am an innocent victim of other people's bad behaviour*. The perfect vicious circle!

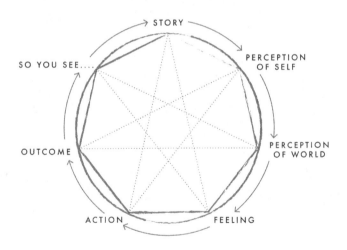

Self-fulfilling prophecy map

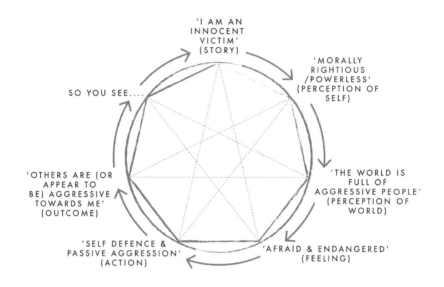

Self-fulfilling prophecy specific example

Using the diagram above, see if you can track one of your own self-fulfilling prophecies. When I discovered this mechanism, I was both deeply sad and elated – sad because of all the precious life energy I had poured into this theatre piece, trying my best to get the 'bad people' to change their ways, i.e. doing the same thing and expecting different results, and elated because now I saw my part in the game, I knew I had the power to change it.

Getting to know your Inner Shaman's resources and being willing to be creative with them makes it much more likely that you will be able to step out of the reactive response to the many triggers in life. In shamanism, we call these triggers *allies*, because if we are willing, they reveal the healing that is ours to do.

In neuroscience, picking out the proof for our own point of view to the exclusion of everything else is called *inattentional blindness*. For the Inner Shaman, recognizing the power our story has to change our perception is actually very good news. If our perception is driven by the meaning we give to our condition, fed by unowned emotion and held in place by our posture, then change any one of these and our perception can change too.

The more we use the tools we have available to embody and own our emotions, and the more willing we are to self-inspect, the more likely we are to discover the part we have played in any conflict we have experienced in life. Here's an example from one of the Movement Medicine teachers we've trained of how the creativity of the Inner Shaman can help us do that:

It was my first Long Dance ceremony in 2010. I was just recovering from cancer and my last chemotherapy. I was tired, scared and without hair. At the age of 34, I knew not only cancer, but also various kinds of chronic illness, which included back pain that at times was debilitating, despite my young age.

I was carrying a strong story about not being able to be healthy and having very little energy. I remember that when we danced with our ancestors, I began a dialogue about being able to be free to experience more pleasure in my life. I could feel the long line of ancestors, especially women, behind me who hadn't expressed their creative juice, their sexuality, their joy and their wild nature. They all seemed very contained, extremely serious and devoted to martyrdom.

I danced for them, feeling my sadness for their suffering, their losses and sacrifices. I told them I wanted to be free and to express my freedom for them too. I received their blessing and their strength, and it was as if a channel behind me had opened and I felt a change in my body.

I don't know how to describe this without sounding woo-woo, but the back pain I had suffered for many years disappeared that night in an instant and has never returned.

LAURA VALENTI.
MOVEMENT MEDICINE TEACHER AND COACH

It is inevitable and necessary that as part of our journey towards self-knowledge we will spend time in the shadow lands of the human psyche. Knowing what it is to be disempowered, irresponsible and lost in a theatre of selves who are afraid, reactive and fixed humbles us and deepens genuine compassion. To recognize and accept these unowned, unknown parts of ourselves that make up our shadow makes it less likely that we will fall under their spell and project their self-fulfilling prophecies onto the world around us. This is the ongoing work of a lifetime and no amount of spiritual bypassing will help. To become who we are, we have to recognize, embrace and make choices about who we are not. The human ego is a fragile creature and it can cause untold damage when it has its hands on the steering wheel of our choices and actions.

For the Inner Shaman, life is an ongoing invitation to discover and take responsibility for who we are, both shadow and light. When I began working in the Middle East, I witnessed first-hand how all sides in the ongoing struggles there competed to be seen as the righteous victims of one another's bad behaviour. This affected me deeply and I began to see that this blame and counter-blame mode was at the heart of every conflict I witnessed or was involved in. I saw how often I perceived myself as the victim of other people's unconsciousness and I understood how hard it was to see my own part in the creation of every single one of those difficulties. This led me to look at Stephen Karpman's dynamic model of social interaction and conflict called *the drama triangle*. We're going to make use of this work now from a shamanic perspective.

THE (SHAMANIC) DRAMA TRIANGLE

The drama triangle is made up of three well-known characters. Please enter Victim, Persecutor and Rescuer. In our work, we have found it helpful to name a fourth role, the Hungry Ghost. This expands Karpman's drama triangle into a vicious circle whose momentum can devour enormous amounts of life energy. All the roles keep us away from the underlying emotions that they mask. Most of these emotions are rooted in past pain projected onto present circumstances. You will be likely to find, for example, that a Persecutor was once a Victim themselves. But unowned emotion leads to blaming, bullying, self-pity and our human predilection for maintaining the moral high ground by claiming to be the biggest Victim on the block. It is the foundation of our rigid certainties and dismissal of those we do not understand – dismissal that can so easily end in violence. It is present, too, in the spiritual malady of our addictions.

Wherever I travel, I see these roles being played out to devastating effect in our relationships with ourselves, each other and the world we live in. All of them support one another so as to remain convinced of their point of view. The Persecutor needs a Victim to blame. The Rescuer needs a Victim so they can keep the focus off themselves. The Victim needs both Rescuer and the Persecutor to keep them powerless and locked into the story that nothing can change. And the Hungry Ghost sits on a dark whirlpool of ancient emotion that feeds this vicious circle and keeps it turning at speed, sucking the life out of us and keeping us locked into our suffering.

Over the years, I've developed a way of working with these characters that leads into working with the shadow. In my experience, shadows can and do show up in all areas of life – money, sex, power, you name it. I've found it enormously fruitful and life-benefitting to actively seek out my own shadows. I'm confident you will too.

The Inner Shaman is a fine ally in this. Their love of the unknown and intrinsic creativity are invaluable at those inevitable times in life when the lights go out and we find ourselves stumbling in the dark. So it's time now to ask your Inner Shaman to help you acknowledge and own how the roles of Victim, Persecutor, Rescuer and Hungry Ghost operate in your life as a vicious circle and collectively make up the central villain of the piece, the Charlatan or False Self, who is guaranteed to cause you and others pain.

As a way out of this circle, we will invoke and embody the four archetypal presences that make up the medicine circle: the Dancing Warrior, the Dancing Fool, the Wise Elder and the Wounded Healer. These four medicine archetypes are powerful allies who collectively empower our central archetype, the nemesis of the Charlatan, the Inner Shaman. Their mutually enhancing skills will give you the resources to see how the vicious circle operates, escape from it and step into the medicine circle. That is the intention of this practice.

🌿 PRACTICE: FROM VICIOUS CIRCLE 🌿
TO MEDICINE CIRCLE – CREATING NEW GROUND

Timing

You will need an hour for this practice.

Preparation

As preparation for this powerful ritual, take some time to read the descriptions of the characters involved in the vicious circle (*below*) and the medicine circle (*p.135*) and contemplate how they relate to your life.

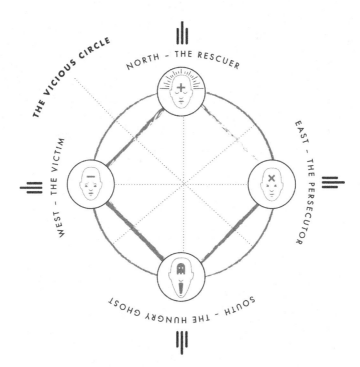

The characters of the vicious circle

South: The Hungry Ghost

The Hungry Ghost is well known to most of us in one form or another. They play out our collective story that there is something missing inside us that can be described as a lack of both genuine nurturing (mothering) and loving discipline (fathering). Not knowing their own ground, the Hungry Ghost seeks to find it in whatever their hunger attaches to. Deep down, self-loathing, shame and a genuine lack of confidence in themselves and in life are the poisoned ground they stand on. They seek external approval and external solutions and at the same time, even if they are received, they will never be enough. The spiritual malady of addiction leads them on a downward spiral where the only respite is the fleeting pleasure of surrender to their addiction followed swiftly by a temporary zoning out from the suffering of life that only adds to the malaise on their return.

East: The Persecutor

The Persecutor condemns and blames the Victim and has no problem letting them know it. They use their power to make sure that *everyone* realizes Victims are to blame for their own troubles. After all, they are bad people and, in the extreme, not even worthy members of the human race. Persecutors are righteously convinced that they are doing what's best, and as long as it benefits them, they maintain the status quo, claiming it to be the natural order of things. But deep down, they are lonely, and behind their iron mask, they are secretly longing for love.

West: The Victim

The Victim feels powerless to engage creatively with life. They take the moral high ground but play low status, and because they see themselves as weak, they don't notice the effect they are having on others and their environment. They say: 'Life is happening to me, just as it always has, just as it always will.' They wear their past hurts as good reason not to take responsibility for themselves in the present. They justify their behaviour by staying identified with being powerless to change it in any way. Deep down, they are afraid of the fury they are sitting on, and though they depend on their Rescuer, resentment is never far away.

North: The Rescuer

The Rescuer, the classic do-gooding enabler, works to keep the focus off themselves at all costs. They have convinced themselves that they can and must save Victims from Persecutors. They see exactly what needs to happen and they impose their view on the situation without being asked. In so doing, they manage both to enrage the Persecutor and keep the Victim feeling as powerless as ever. Deep down, they believe that if they give enough, eventually someone will love them back. A common phrase for Rescuers is: 'After all I've done for you, this is what I get.' From there, it's only a short hop into any of the other roles in the vicious circle.

✐ Now let's explore the four archetypal allies who can support your Inner Shaman in shifting from vicious circle to medicine circle. As you read, ask yourself how familiar you are with them and what may help you to fruitfully engage with them.

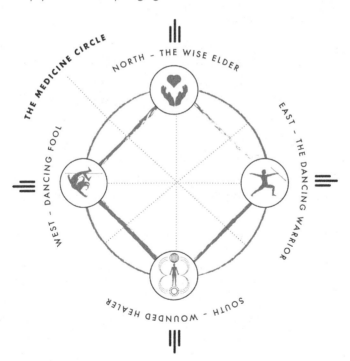

The characters of the medicine circle

South: The Wounded Healer

The Wounded Healer, rooted in our connection to the Divine Mother and Divine Father, is hugely important to our wellbeing on every level. Whatever our experience with our own parents, the archetypal mama offers the warm holding, safety and acceptance vital to healthy beginnings, while the archetypal papa offers the clear, loving and boundaried guidance that gives us the safety and confidence to know where we are and grow into who we are. Whatever our personal history, we can all make a connection with the Divine Mother in the form of the Earth under our feet and the Divine Father in the form of the light of the sun. Together, they make up the archetype of the Wounded Healer, who can provide the nurturing and illumination we need to choose a path of self-acceptance and self-determination and break the chains of our addictions.

East: The Dancing Warrior

The Dancing Warrior uses the very same power that the Persecutor uses to stand up for and protect what matters most to them and to fight for what they hold most valuable. Without a doubt, owning who we are in this world and facing the unknown that is so much part of life in a body require the power and discipline of a Warrior. The Holy Grail for the Warrior is the power of choice. They don't indulge the omnipotent fantasy that we create reality, but they understand that we do create our *perception* of reality. They provide the protection that we need to feel safe enough to recognize the inherent vulnerability of being human.

West: The Dancing Fool

The Dancing Fool is creativity itself. Without past or future there is only the invitation of the present. Laughter and play are good medicine. Even more so is that quiet awe in the face of the improbable magnificence of existence that opens our eyes to the mystery and gives the Dancing Fool the power to fully embrace the opportunity of the moment. Their fascination with life allows them to see the ingredients on offer in any given situation as a rich palette of colour with which to create. Their imagination is boundless and their fear non-existent. Their innocence is their protection and the world their oyster.

North: The Wise Elder

The Wise Elder is the part of us who witnesses all of life's happenings with the love, patience and depth born of long-term practice. They have been with us through all the ups and downs of life, sitting quietly at the centre of our heart, waiting for us to come and join them and ask them for guidance. They hold our inner wisdom. They take the long view that eldership brings. They know us well and they have that humorous twinkle in their eye and wrinkled smile that hint at golden secrets.

Practice

✍ Okay, now let's take this into movement. As always, *Awakening the Dancer (p.29)* is the place to begin. Acknowledge your condition and invoke your support. You need free-moving energy and active physicality and imagination to do this practice effectively. Check that you feel fully present and focused on your intention for this ritual. Move with one of the earlier practices until you do.

✍ Once your body is warm, take some time for the ancient shamanic practice called *shaking medicine*. Animals shake when they need to release fear or excess adrenaline from their system, as we saw with the deer earlier. Let your animal body remember how to do this *as if* you were needing to release yourself from something. Don't push, but invite your body to vibrate and shake from the inside. Take care of yourself. Mobilize your joints. (Five minutes minimum.)

✍ We will begin with the roles of the vicious circle. Be prepared for part of you to feel embarrassed, but remember that this ritual has the purpose of taking you beyond the mask that is usually in place behind your everyday consciousness. You may even surprise yourself and enjoy the process of recognizing and embodying these roles in the drama of your life. As you work with them, try not to judge them too harshly. They are all reactions to pain. What feelings are they protecting you from? How do you move from one role to the next? How do they support one another in keeping you locked into this vicious circle? How does this play out in your day-to-day life? I suggest taking a couple of minutes for each of the shadow roles plus five minutes to explore how you move from one to another. If you run into difficulties, slow down, pause and call in more resources. The Dancing Warrior in you knows when help is needed and always has the courage to ask for it.

South: The Hungry Ghost

✍ To begin, invite the dancer to step into the South of your circle and to show you through shape and repetition how the Hungry Ghost acts out through you. Be aware of its posture, movement and expression. Use the connection to the elements that is natural to the Inner Shaman to be as creative as you can be. What does the Hungry Ghost feel? Notice how they lack any sense of nurturing and how their weakness will seem to cloud their power to choose. What is the emptiness inside that they feel compelled to fill with their addictions?

✍ Once you feel ready, shake yourself free of this expression, just as a butterfly shakes before leaving its cocoon. Well done. Please don't make the mistake of imagining that the Hungry Ghost will never get hold of you again. You are doing this practice to acknowledge its existence – but also to strengthen that quiet voice inside you that will remind you that you have a choice the next time you fall into this role.

East: The Persecutor

✍ Next, step into the East of your circle and do the same work with the Persecutor. Remember that the Persecutor blames and criticizes. This energy can be directed at others or yourself. In this ritual, we are focusing on how the Persecutor is your own worst critic and will use anything to lock you into the vicious cycle of blaming and shaming. See how they use anger to blame others. And notice how secretly, behind their armour, they long for love. How does the Persecutor show up in you? What effect do they have?

🖋 Once you've explored this, shake yourself free again.

West: The Victim

🖋 Next, step into the West of your circle and embody the Victim. Remember that the Victim feels powerless. They will not take any responsibility for what is happening. Notice how they use your past experiences as an excuse for your behaviour in the present. Under this, there is passive aggression, and under that, fury. Can you feel it? Can you give yourself permission to own it? Embodied fury is the key that will open the door if you let the Victim know that they are safe to express it and break free.

🖋 When you see everything through this lens, what do you notice? You may feel saddened to witness times in your life when you have been a genuine victim of circumstance or the unconscious abuse of power that is part of our world in so many ways. Acknowledge this and try to see the difference between your actual experience and how the Victim uses your personal history to keep you powerless and attached to the meaning you have so far made of your life.

🖋 Call your resources, shake yourself free and continue.

North: The Rescuer

🖋 Next, step into the North of your circle and embody the Rescuer. They feel sorry for the Victim, blame the Persecutor and do everything they can to keep the focus away from themselves. They arrogantly *know* what the Victim needs, so they don't listen, just impose their own remedy. Notice how the Rescuer operates through you. Don't mistake them for the part of you that generously, heartfully wants to help out a friend or offer something of beauty to the world. The difference is subtle, but of massive importance. As a friend, you listen. If you have advice to offer, you offer it without attachment to it being correct or received. How does the Rescuer show up in you?

🖎 Shake yourself free and come back to the centre of your circle.

Centre: The Charlatan

🖎 At the centre of the vicious circle you will find its source, *the Charlatan*, an imposter who claims to have a special skill or truth. The Charlatan's only genuine skill is playing out the postures, stories and expectations of the ego. They are the quintessential false self, disconnected from reality and locked inside a prison of their own making. Take some time to embody this very human condition. The Charlatan came into being to protect your essential self. They played a role for you and have simply forgotten how and why they came into being.

🖎 Once again, shake yourself free and come back to the centre of your circle and then say these words, or your own version of them, out loud:

> *I am not these roles or their shadows. They operate through me. They are doing their best to protect me and, step by step, with all the help I can get, I am on my way to acknowledging them and releasing any hold they have over me.*

Well done. That's brave work. By stepping into these roles, you have begun the process of disidentifying from them.

The medicine archetypes

It's time now to work with the four medicine archetypes. These are powerful allies who collectively empower the central archetype, the nemesis of the Charlatan, the Inner Shaman.

✍ Take them one by one, stepping into their direction:

~ South to the Wounded Healer

~ East to the Dancing Warrior

~ West to the Dancing Fool

~ North to the Wise Elder

Feel them inside you, shape them, animate them in movement, see how they strengthen the Inner Shaman's way of embodying the power of choice (the Dancing Warrior), creativity (the Dancing Fool), love (the Wise Elder) and self-care and self-determination (the Wounded Healer). You may be more familiar with one and less familiar with another. Notice this as potential space to grow into as you deepen your relationship with them through practice. As you move from one archetype to another, take time to explore how their individual and collective strengths may help you to step out of the vicious circle and into the medicine circle.

✍ Complete this by returning to the Inner Shaman at the centre of your circle. Take some time to experience the considerable extra support that these archetypes have now brought to your circle.

Intent incantations

✍ The next step is the culmination of this ritual. You are learning new skills and creating new pathways inside your psyche. Find a simple distilled movement, emotional quality and phrase for each medicine archetype; for example: 'I am the Dancing Warrior in Ya'Acov. I am the remembrance of choice. I own the Fire of my anger and channel its power to protect what I love.' We call these embodied statements of intent *incantations*. Over time, through using them, we can change the focus of our unconscious internal dialogue so that our self-talk and actions become congruent with our aspiration to be who we truly are. One incantation for each archetype is good. Let them develop over the days, weeks and months ahead. As you work with these archetypes, they will become more and more available to you when you need them.

✍ Complete the ritual in the normal way, making sure to write down your incantations and anything else you wish to remember.

✍ It is also very helpful to find a simple action that puts your incantation into practice. For instance, if I found an incantation connected with the creativity of the Dancing Fool, something like 'My creativity is a source of everyday joy and empowerment for me', I would then make sure I set five minutes aside twice a week to do something creative that had no other purpose than grounding this incantation in my day-to-day life. Incantations are like seeds. Taking a simple action that confirms an incantation is like planting that seed and watering it, so that in time it will grow into its full potential.

❦❦❦❦

Before we leave this chapter, I won't be able to look my wife in the eye if I don't confess that the characters in the vicious circle can still take me over from time to time. It's never pretty. And the witness in me watches in amused, pained and loving disbelief as there I go again, pointing the finger of blame, rushing in to save someone from their own suffering, feeling weak and powerless to change anything and reaching outside myself to anything I can find to feed the insatiable hunger inside. However, I can no longer do this without that strong voice inside warning me to stop *now* before I do any damage!

It takes a lot of repetition to create an unhealthy habit and a lot of repetition to replace it with a healthy one. That's the purpose of practising something – to get good at it. With practice and support, any of us can shift the balance of power in our psyche and spend more time in the best version of ourselves we can be.

I've found this kind of work has made me more sensitive to what is true for me and more able to express it. And shadow work, which we have begun with this ritual, can be extremely energizing and even enjoyable!

Congratulations. Your Inner Shaman now has four archetypes around them that will make them stronger and more resourced. You now have everything in place to complete your basket full of medicine with some shamanic alchemy. Time to transform a little lead into gold!

CHAPTER 9

Lead into Gold

The Alchemy of Movement Medicine

*'That's what alchemists do. They show that
when we strive to become better than we are,
everything around us becomes better, too.'*

PAOLO COELHO

Now that the Inner Shaman has their helpers in place, we can turn our attention to their alchemical expertise and the power we all have within us to transform lead into gold. The lead we are talking about here is the weight of our undigested personal and collective histories. In a day-to-day sense, it can simply be the weight of a difficult day or experience. The gold we are seeking is the gold of present moment awareness through which we can relax into the arms of a greater power.

Ancient alchemists were seeking gold because of its stability. Once gold is gold, you can do what you like to it. Freeze it, melt it, chop it into pieces – whatever you do, gold is gold is gold. If you apply this to the psyche, alchemists are looking for the stable, we might say Unbroken, gold of the soul. For the Inner Shaman, who must often travel to the unpredictable land of the unknown, gold is the self-knowledge that enables them to withstand that pressure and return safely. Don Juan, the old Yaqui medicine man from the Carlos Castaneda tales, used to say that people were often surprised when the doors to the unknown opened. He would laugh, saying that people seeking freedom would approach those doors, and when they opened and they saw the vastness of the unknown staring back at them, most would run for their lives.

Gabrielle used to tell us all the time, 'Teachers come and go, but life is the master.' We call this master intelligence in life *the Great Choreographer*. I have noticed again and again how, with impeccable timing, life puts the people and situations in front of me to deliver just what I need to become a little more conscious of who I am. Imagine how your life might be if you acted as if each significant encounter you had was a direct invitation to look in the universal mirror and know yourself more deeply. Batty Thunder Bear, one of my original teachers, used to tell his apprentices that ultimately, there was no inherent universal meaning in our existence. However, we humans are meaning makers and storytellers, and we do derive meaning from our experience. So, he asked us to seek out and choose meaning for our lives that empowered us, so that waking up in the morning, no matter the external reality of our situation, was simply another invitation to create with the raw materials at hand.

We have seen how much power the story we tell has in creating our perception of ourselves, each other and the situations life puts us in. If I can choose the meaning that I give to my life as a whole and to each situation as it arises, then I can become what shamans have always been – a master of perception. I've tried this out in all sorts of unlikely situations, and it works.

For example, I was once arrested in South Dakota for speeding on my way to catch a flight home. I was late, and in my hurry, I'd rather stupidly lost awareness of my speed. Whoops! Not only that, I was in an open-top sports car and had a copy of Russell Means' excellent autobiography, *Where White Men Fear to Tread,* on the front seat next to me. Russell was a political and spiritual leader of the Lakota people who had a fearsome reputation and in his constant search for justice for his people was a constant thorn in the side of the authorities.

Suffice to say that the white policeman who stopped me wasn't one of Russell's greatest fans. He picked the book up, saw that it was a signed copy and before I knew it, my luggage and car were impounded, my shoelaces and belt removed, and I was in the back of a police car, my arms handcuffed behind my back, being driven at breakneck speed to the South Dakota State Penitentiary. When I explained to my arresting officer that I had to catch my flight to get back for work, he seemed to take great pleasure in telling me that not only would I now miss my flight, I would almost certainly be spending the next three nights in prison due to it being a holiday weekend.

I was shocked by the sudden change in my situation. My heart was pounding, sweat was stinging my eyes and my mind was leaping into all the repercussions of missing my flight. My inner Persecutor was out of his cage, too, putting the words of a meme I'd recently posted right in front of me and mocking me with them:

Your story is mostly an unconscious set of expectations and beliefs about who you are and what life is. In any challenging situation, being aware that there might be a story operating creates the possibility of perceiving beyond it.

'Okay,' I said to myself, 'let's see if this shamanic alchemy shit works.'

I quietly called my allies, the Tree of Life, the elements, the whole crew. The Inner Shaman's way of working with alchemy involves five simple steps, each one related to an element:

1. *Earth – Presence:* This is the art of being in the Earth of the body and heart, quieting the mind and being with the reality of what is happening as it is happening. The Inner Shaman knows how to focus their attention on what is happening and in doing so interrupt the mind's ability to cloud the situation with overwhelming fears, which so often leads to dissociation, the direct opposite of presence. The ability to dissociate is a powerful survival mechanism when we are powerless to protect ourselves or make any change. But we have been learning ways to tolerate being present and embodied, even in very challenging situations. Being in the body and connected to the Earth grounds our thinking and gives us access to a feeling of safety that calms down our nervous system, opens our awareness to a wider picture and ultimately helps us to make better choices.

2. *Fire – Expression:* This is invoking the Fire within to help us find the courage to express, in shape, movement and breath, what is happening, especially emotionally. I hope that the importance of letting emotions move is now clearer to you. Fire's medicine is its ability to transform everything back into its original state, releasing heat and light in the process. This means that the more we know

the Fire within and connect through that to the power of the sun, the greater our capacity to express what needs to be expressed and, in doing so, transform it in the flames.

3. *Water – Release:* Calling the Waters to wash through our body, heart and mind, releasing debris through a little shaking medicine, purifying ourselves, and becoming as fluid as water will stop the old stories taking over and drowning us in their self-fulfilling expectations. The more we deepen our relationship to the Waters of life through our practice and through being grateful for them, the easier it is to identify with their medicine when the need is there.

4. *Air – Receive:* If we have worked successfully with Earth, Fire and Water, then we will have emptied ourselves of any debris and we will naturally come into the hollow bone space and be able to call the spirit of the wind to lift us up, show us the bigger picture and bring in the inspiration of an appropriate new story. Finding new stories that dignify us and release us from the past, supported by the archetypal energies of the medicine circle, is the shaman's way.

5. *Ether – the Echo:* For the Inner Shaman, ether is the force of attraction or the loving intelligence of the divine that keeps the wheel of life turning. It is essentially the emptiness from which all the elements emerged. This empty space allows new learning to bed in and find its ground in both the imaginal and physical worlds. We all need this phase of digesting and resting in *the echo,* and it is an important aspect of integration after any healing process.

Working with Movement Medicine alchemy

In the situation I was in, it was clearly impossible to dance, but I have used this process so often that I knew that I was capable of engaging with it on the micro level without attracting any more unwanted attention. And so I did. Coming into my breath and my body and becoming present helped calm me down. Quietly, I felt the warmth of the sun on my face and inside me. I felt how angry I was, with myself, with my arresting officer, about missing my flight, and, most of all, about not getting home to Susannah. I felt the Fire rising, and as I breathed, small adjustments and imagination aplenty gave me the feeling of that Fire moving through me. I called the Waters and felt the micro shake inside as they washed through me. And then I gave my attention to the wind coming through the patrol car's open windows. I let my spirit climb into the sky, and as I looked down, I saw the big picture. As a white man, I knew that being arrested for speeding wouldn't be life-threatening. Being late for work would be unfortunate but not deadly. And what was life teaching me about trying to fit too much into a busy day and getting myself into a rush? The wind gave me the feeling of space and freedom that I'd always known nobody could take away from me. So then I just sat back, relaxed and let go. The whole thing barely took five minutes, but afterwards, although nothing had changed externally, my whole world looked different. I was curious, unafraid and, remarkably, even enjoying the strange adventure I was in.

The policeman clearly noticed something and began telling me it was his son's birthday and he was upset about having to work and miss the celebrations at home. Five minutes later, we were talking freely about all kinds of things. By the time we arrived at the prison, he was reassuring me that I shouldn't have anything much to worry about.

I had alchemized the heaviness of my situation and the sparkle was back in my eyes. And the reality that unfolded over the next two days was quite different from the one my fears had shown me. A series of mini-miracles and the generosity of many people got me home 20 minutes before my work was due to begin. And I will always remember the kindness and humour of the Lakota guys I shared my cell with. They all knew Russell and were pretty certain that it was his book that had aggravated my arresting officer. So I learned more about their situation. And on my way back home, I made a commitment to slow my driving down and allow more time for the unexpected in my travel plans. Good outcome. Lesson learned.

Of course, there are many more serious challenges in life than this, but it does illustrate that this alchemical process really does work if we are willing to give space to what's actually true and to be open to whatever the Great Choreographer is attempting to teach us. Like any new process, it can be a bit clunky at first. But if there is a way to feel the safety of ground under our feet, practice will lead to results.

Shamans are often called shapeshifters, which honours their ability to change their form in order to move through different worlds. In the modern world, the biggest freedom we have is the freedom to acknowledge, express, release and eventually change and choose the meaning of any situation. That changes the shape of our consciousness and that in turn changes our perception of reality. If we attend to what a situation is teaching us, we will discover the golden seed that becomes part of the stability and power of the Inner Shaman.

Alchemists work with the elements to create just the right amount of pressure in the alchemical container known as the alembic in order to transform the dull metal weight of lead into the shining stability of gold. In life, the alembic is the body. And for alchemy to happen, we have to commit ourselves fully to each stage of the process.

Opposite, you will see the medicine wheel that sums up all the empowerment work we've been doing in this part of the book.

In our last practice in Part II of our journey, I'm going to invite you to work with the five steps of Movement Medicine alchemy. Be patient as you are learning. Feeling incompetent is a sign of being on new ground. To move past feeling like a failure, we have to feed the Fire of our passion, which means understanding why what we are learning matters to us. I've given you many reasons why I think this work matters. I'm sure you'll have your own. The deeper you go, the clearer you must become about your own motivation.

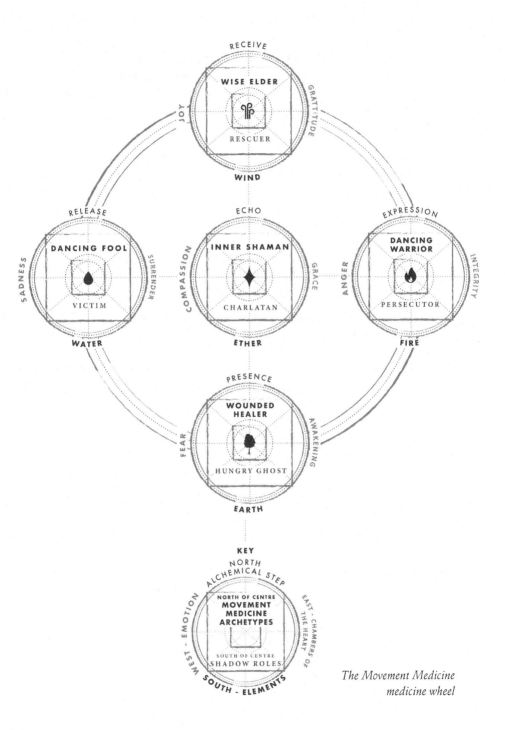

The Movement Medicine
medicine wheel

❧ PRACTICE: LEAD INTO GOLD ❧
– THE ALCHEMY OF MOVEMENT MEDICINE

Timing

How long you take for this ritual will depend on the subject you choose to work with. It's a good idea to start with a minor irritation rather than a hugely challenging issue.

Preparation

⬿ Choose a specific issue. This could be something that has upset you in the last week or a challenge you've faced at work or with a friend or colleague. When other people are involved, remember that you're looking for the meaning you're making, rather than blaming someone else for your condition.

⬿ Prepare yourself and your space in the normal way and call in all the support that is now available to you. Connect as strongly as you can in movement with the Inner Shaman and their allies.

Practice

⬿ Once you feel ready to begin, follow the five steps of the alchemy process (above). As you do so, beware of old ideas that may tell you that you're not capable of doing this. And beware of the characters from the vicious circle getting hold of your work. If they do, use what you now know to give them space to move and then return as soon as you can to your focus. Remember that emotional expression is like weather, and thunder and lightning are sometimes necessary to clear out your heart.

⬿ When you get to the last step, if you don't feel you've finished the process, be prepared to go round the circle again and give more space to your heart and to what you feel. I'm confident that you have it within you to do what is necessary to transform a spoonful of lead into a spoonful of gold!

✍ Complete your ritual in the normal way, making sure to leave enough time for the echo.

❦❦❦❦

Congratulations. You now have enough medicine in your basket to empower your Inner Shaman to transform your world. Take a moment to study the medicine wheel before moving on.

So far, you've been gathering power through your work. The next stage of your journey will focus on taking responsibility for that power.

PART III

~

RESPONSIBILITY

A Bridge across the Arc of Time

'The time is always right to do what is right.'

Martin Luther King, Jr

For the Inner Shaman, responsibility isn't a weight to be carried, but the joy of living life with a self-chosen and meaningful purpose. This part of our journey is all about how we take responsibility for the power we have gathered and learn to use it in alignment with who we are and what we wish to create. For the Inner Shaman, this means understanding and working with the direct connection between the past, present and future and creating a bridge across what we call *the arc of time*.

Some years ago, I was teaching a workshop that was focused on deepening our relationship with our ancestors. Towards the end of the weekend, I heard my own ancestors whispering to me as I danced: 'Ya'Acov, all this work with the past is a wonderful thing and we are delighted to be honoured and welcomed in this way. But you haven't yet asked the most important question.'

'Oh, what's that?'

Their answer touched me and has stayed with me ever since. 'What kind of ancestor will you be? What will you pass on?'

The choices we make today are already the inheritance of the generations that will follow. Every choice we make that is unconsciously motivated by past hurt or unexamined and inaccurate assumptions will keep the vicious circle of blame and counter-blame spinning. The world is full of conflicts that began hundreds and even thousands of years ago, conflicts in which each side is certain that the other is solely to blame. This is the height of irresponsibility and is a destructive use of power.

Responsibility means healing the pain we carry, and healing means choosing to break the chains of suffering inside us, between us and between us and the rest of the web of life on the planet. It means forgiveness. Not 'words only, sugar on shit' forgiveness, but the full-hearted, full-bodied, clear-minded forgiveness that comes from being willing to acknowledge the truth, learn from it and move forward.

It doesn't mean being perfect. Even the most accomplished of Persian carpet weavers follows the tradition of deliberately making one mistake in their carpets. They call it the *spirit stitch* and they include it in recognition that 'only Allah is perfect'. How beautiful is that? And making mistakes, as I can say from experience, is one of the ways we learn. Shamanism is rooted in learning through trial and error. There's a thin line between fantasy and clear guidance, and we learn to discern which is which by carefully considering the outcomes of inspirations born in the altered state of ritual. In this way, we can be responsible for our choices and adjust them as we learn more.

The Inner Shaman is aware that a better future on Earth will only be possible for us if enough of us make the choice to heal the past and gain a deeper understanding of our place here. It's a matter of developing a more embodied consciousness. By the time we complete our work together, it's my intention that you will know your Inner Shaman's predilection for using all the material that life provides to create as much beauty and medicine as possible from it.

All the shamans I know have the shine in their eyes that comes from travelling back and forth across the arc of time. They experience the connection between their life now and their ancestors' lives, and they have a vision of a future in which life continues to evolve for their descendants. And because they know the fragility and the impermanence of physical life, they seize the gift of it with both hands while they can. They seek that fierce blend of self-acceptance and discipline that leads to personal power and assuming responsibility for that power.

Personal power isn't based on what others think about us or the cards that life has dealt us. It doesn't come through our position in the world, but from the self-knowledge that comes from self-development. With personal power, we can honour our ancestors' experiences and our own, and not be limited by either. Personal power comes from the medicine we have made from those experiences. Choosing to use our personal power in service of the deepest truth inside us, and with the future of our descendants in mind, is the art of taking responsibility for our life.

So, with the Inner Shaman's help, in chapters 10 and 11, we will look at developing self-responsibility; in Chapter 12, the focus is on being responsible in relationships; and in Chapter 13, on updating our vision of a joyfully responsible and fulfilling relationship with the community of life. A universal shamanic principle is the simple acknowledgement that the work we do in ritual is 'for all our relations'. That includes everything behind us and in front of us, everything around us, above us, below us, inside us and beyond us. It's a simple and powerful way of acknowledging interconnection and it reminds us of the wider context of our existence.

When we are who we are, we transform our world. I hear life asking us all to stand up now, hold our heads high and commit to making a difference in the world. Now is the time. Benevolent Death is always at our side, reminding us that now is all we ever have. That reminder sharpens my intent to fully enjoy this gift called life in a body on Earth while I can.

Research shows that true contentment comes from giving what is ours to give. We have mostly ignored that and tried consuming our way to happiness instead. Not only has this failed, it's also created a vast amount of mindless destruction. We need to take responsibility for this and use our power in a different way. It won't be an easy shift. But I believe every generation has had the challenge of dreaming a better dream. And as a species, on our journey through time we have accumulated power, artistry and imagination. We all have it within us to be noble and generous, cruel and irresponsible. It's a choice we remain free to make.

Through my work as a shaman I've discovered who I am and what my responsibilities to life are. I've made my choice. I know that your Inner Shaman can help you to do the same. If your heart is still beating, then the doors remain open. Shall we?

Chapter 10

Real Spirits and Imaginary Friends

Finding Ground in the Imaginal World

*'I have fallen in love with the imagination.
And if you fall in love with the imagination,
you understand that it is a free spirit. It will
go anywhere, and it can do anything.'*

Alice Walker

As you work with your Inner Shaman, it's possible, even probable, that you'll come up against scepticism, either from others or from yourself. This is normal. We live in a world that has made the rational mind the emperor, so we are bound to question any other perception of reality. I trust the spirits that guide me and when I am working in ritual or healing space, doubt is in the background, where it needs to be. But I've come to realize that without the allies of doubt, critical thinking and the checks and balances of elders and mentors, there is only certainty. And certainty closes the door on other possibilities and leads to the desert of dogma. So I've learned to nurture my doubts and to flirt with uncertainty. The Inner Shaman is no stranger to charisma and power, and they are a heady blend that can lead to self-importance. And we've all seen what happens to those who believe their own press. Over the years, I've made it my business to seek out people of power who have remained humble, teachable and challengeable as their mojo grows. They do exist and the fact that there is a paucity of such people in the world is a sobering reality check.

I've come to recognize that the more connected I feel to the spirits that guide me and the more I learn to trust them, the more I need my rational mind, and my human friends and teachers as mirrors once the ceremony is over. I take note that the elder shamans we know and love in the Amazon, who have been leading ceremonies for more than 60 years, still have their teachers.

Not long ago, I was in a taxi in slow-moving traffic with a young Algerian driver called Mourad. He asked me what I did for a living and I told him. He was curious. His grandmother had worked with herbs and he remembered people coming from far and wide to seek her help. He asked me about my beliefs and I told him that what I believed in most was the Mystery. Then he asked how I prayed, so I told him, 'Sometimes I light a fire and drum. I dance and sing and the warmth of the fire touches the Fire inside me, and through that I feel a connection to the Great Light that feeds our sun. I express whatever is in my heart, and in the emptiness that follows, I receive guidance. I hear words or see images or feel a sensation in my body. And when that guidance touches my heart in a way that rings true with me, I find that my will surrenders to a kind of divine obedience that I have learned over the years to trust.'

Mourad was silent for a while. Then he said softly, 'How do you know that what you hear isn't just what you want to hear? How can you trust it? When I pray, I only repeat the words of the Prophet. I only have to follow the words of the Koran and all will be well.'

I felt the passion and the power of his faith. They touched me and I told him so. He smiled. And then he continued, 'What book do you follow? How can you be sure that your voice from the fire or guidance from your spirits will lead you on a good road and not away from God?'

'I can't be sure. Shamanism isn't a religion based on belief, but a way of experiencing the divine through embodied connection with the powers of nature and the spirits. That, alongside the guidance of my elders and teachers, is the book I follow. To me, nature is the physical intelligence of the Creator. It is a pure mirror. Nothing in nature is trying to be anything other than what it is. And therefore when I look in that mirror, I see reflected back to me what is true within me and what is false. When I take the time to ask for this mirroring, nature is always generous.'

'But what if nature told you to harm someone, even your enemy? How can you trust something as changeable and varied as nature?'

'I've never been asked to do anything that is against my own nature,' I replied. 'And I have checks and balances that I use to help me. I ask my wife, my elders and my mentors for their reflections. I listen. And often I adjust my view accordingly. Sometimes I have to go back to my spirits and dialogue with them. It's a process. I know there have been many "messages from spirits" that have turned out to be plain psychosis. And there are spirits of all kinds hanging out wanting to be heard and there's no guarantee that their guidance will be any wiser than the guidance of a stranger on the street. Or in a taxi, for that matter.'

He laughed.

'That's why,' I continued, 'knowing ourselves and taking responsibility for our decisions are so important in shamanism. I know my own intentions and the spirits who have become my guides are with me because they have the same intentions. We are partners in a shared project.'

'I'm sorry,' Mourad replied, 'that you're having to rely on imaginary friends and human beings for advice.'

I laughed.

We said goodbye as brothers on different roads and there was genuine warmth between us.

If you were to ask me, 'Are your spirits real or are they imaginary friends?', my most honest answer would be: 'The Shaman in me knows they are real. My rational mind questions what "real" means. And my heart is in love with the Mystery of life. I've learned that doubt and patience are good things. And that the more powerfully myself I become, the more I need the human mirroring of those I've asked to keep their beautifully beady eyes on me and challenge me when I go too far off-piste.'

I've also found it useful to recognize that in the spirit world, visions and dreams can appear fully formed at the speed of our imagination. So, in my earlier years of working, I often made the mistake of thinking that because my visions were so real to me, they would be easy to bring down to Earth. But we need to give some consideration to the density of the physical world. I've had to learn that being embodied means moving more slowly than my mind and working with the world of physical limitations. As a species, we may have to learn this too, or be stopped in our tracks.

Evolution is a regular updating of our underlying story. I encourage you to regularly ask your Inner Shaman what updates they suggest for you. I know that my own life would be much the poorer if I didn't do this. Regular ritual has taught me to see my life as one long creative project, and I've found there's enormous satisfaction in seeing how my dreams take form over time.

NO SPACE FOR SQUATTERS

Shamanism is a blend of step-by-step care and the free-form surrender of dancing on the edge between the known and the unknown. People often ask me about the dangers of working in this way. After all, there are all kinds of mischievous and unhelpful beings in the imaginal realms, just as there are anywhere else. I admit, I used to feel critical of those who experienced the drama of 'psychic attacks'. I always felt that they were using the feeling of being attacked to avoid taking responsibility for a snake pit of unowned personal emotion. I had to learn, through a good slice of humble pie, that these attacks do have an external reality. So, I was wrong, but I was also right in that there is always an element of personal story, as I will explain below. Where I've got to is recognizing that having good boundaries in the shamanic realm and protecting ourselves properly are important.

How do we protect ourselves? The best way I know is to commit 100 per cent to doing our own personal work and to making sure that we take care of all the basics whenever we enter the realm of the unknown. Most importantly, it means occupying our own physical body and doing our own inner shadow work. If I am fully present in my body, aware of my heart and have set up a strong circle before I work, then there is no space for squatters. At the same time, we all have an unconscious and, therefore, there will be gaps. What I have come to understand and find most helpful in this arena is the understanding that any shadows that try to enter my circle are mirrors of things inside me that I have not yet owned and accepted. I have learned not to be naïve and at the same time not to be paranoid. In this way, I can see my own experiences in this area of attachments and attacks as teaching situations.

There are two main things to learn. First, the importance of ongoing shadow work to own what we have been unconscious of. And second, the importance of having clearly stated and defined boundaries. Finally, I've come to realize that the only power these kinds of energies have is the power we give them. I suggest that you move forward with care, work more with *the Mesa Practice (p.69)* and *Your Animal Heart (p.118)*, and if and when you feel the need, look for some good human guidance from someone further down the road than you.

The deeper you go, the more important your relationship to your allies becomes. There are many kinds of allies in the shaman's world.

You already know the elemental spirits. There are also animal allies and spirit guides who have more human form. There are many kinds of nature spirits, like tree spirits, plant spirits and spirits that are connected to special places like waterfalls. And there are archetypal allies such as the medicine archetypes and Benevolent Death.

For many years, I knew that I had help, but it was unspecific. It was only when Matthis Pentha, a Sami shaman and a dear mentor of mine for many years, asked me, 'Who are your spirits?' that I realized that although I felt their presence, I didn't have any kind of personal relationship with them. So, I set out to find out who they were, using the practices I've already shared with you. In Chapter 14, I'll share some more guidance on how to come into personal relationship with your own guiding spirits. For now, making it clear that you wish to know your guiding spirits and working thoroughly and deeply with the practices I have shared with you up until now will make your circle strong enough for you to continue your development.

Now you've reached this point in your practice where you've gathered some power, I invite you to make the commitment to going deeper by undertaking a profound ritual enquiry. This will involve focusing on a *Nine-Step Checks and Balances Guide for the Inner Shaman* over the next 21 days. First, let's spend some time together in a quiet, slow ritual space, designed to keep you alert and safe as our journey continues, then we'll go on to work specifically with your biography and hunt for the considerable life energy that is locked up there. Remember the resources that are available to your Inner Shaman and remember the Unbroken intelligence of life that is movement and you won't go far off-course.

🌿 PRACTICE: A NINE-STEP CHECKS AND 🌿 BALANCES GUIDE FOR THE INNER SHAMAN

I suggest that you do this enquiry at a time when you can spend 21 minutes a day for 21 consecutive days on it. On Day 1, set up your space, read through the nine steps below and set your personal intention for this work. From Day 2 to Day 19, spend two days with each step until you've done all nine. Spend Day 20 integrating whatever you've learned and then on Day 21 dedicate the totality of your work to the safe and ongoing development of your shamanic practice over the years to come.

If doing this over 21 days isn't possible, find your own timing and work with each of the nine steps. The intention is to build solid foundations for your ongoing practice by committing to making it as safe and responsible as possible, so that your creativity and adventure with the Inner Shaman can flower.

1. Ruthless, kind and ongoing self-inspection

There's no replacement for recognizing that we all have major blind spots and no matter how awake we are, we always will. Our unconscious isn't a bad thing, though – it's all potential wisdom. Go on discovering what your imagination is dedicated to and keep deepening that knowledge through congruent action.

✍ When we state our intentions out loud in ritual, we are taking a powerful step. If you are willing, state your commitment to ruthless, kind and ongoing self-inspection.

2. Gather a circle of human support

We need good mirrors – people who have nothing to lose from telling us the truth as they see it. Look into what qualities you want to see in any elders, mentors and teachers you might invite to be part of your circle of support. Then go ahead and invite them to support you. Check in with them regularly, especially if you're feeling really good and confident.

✍ In ritual, name your elders, mentors and teachers or state your intention to find them.

3.   Become the master of your own circle

The Mesa Practice (p.69) is particularly good for strengthening both our interoception and our boundaries. In ritual, if you ever feel the presence of any energy you're unsure of, ask: 'Are you here for my highest good?' If you don't get an immediate 'yes', respectfully and clearly send that energy away using clear movement, breath and voice if necessary.

✍ Take some time to practise the Mesa work now and to practise your clear 'No!' and your clear 'Yes!' State your clear intention to protect yourself and keep safe on your journey. You don't leave your front door open all the time. Being closed is good. Being open is good too. What we want is the ability to open and close appropriately.

4.   Move beyond naivety

The last step will have reminded you of the need to protect yourself and stay alert when you are working shamanically by yourself. Always be willing to say 'No!' and if you ever feel unsafe, take a step back and gather more resources before moving forward again.

✍ Take some time now to remember the shadow archetypes and their medicine helpers. State your clear intention to check the guidance you receive with people you can trust. Statements like 'Spirit told me to...' need to be checked with human beings who can uphold and challenge you where necessary.

5.   Discover your Inner Shaman's allies and deepen your relationship with them

✍ Begin with the elemental powers. Bringing objects from nature, like a stone or a beautifully shaped small branch, into your ritual space will make your connection to the elementals more personal. Always introduce yourself, share your intention and ask for permission first.

🖎 Then, in ritual space, ask: 'Who are my spirits?'

🖎 Perhaps most importantly, there will be your ancestors and descendants. Making space for them in your circle is important and I believe that we are much the poorer for the lack of attention we give to them in the modern world. Take time to acknowledge them and then invite those ancestors and descendants (whether you have your own children or not) who love and support you to be with you.

We inherit the strength, wisdom and experience of our ancestors. We also inherit their undigested experiences. The more we learn through epigenetics (the passing on of traits) and the study of trans-generational trauma, the more we are coming to understand how the past lives on through us in the present. From the shamanic perspective, this is good news. The more life energy is locked in the past, the more potential energy is available to us now.

🖎 Spend some time simply being in the power of the imaginal space. Tell your allies what really matters to you. Have a dialogue with them. Then, once you have said all you need to say, release them.

6.   Treat everyone as autonomous

Never try to make changes on behalf of anyone unless they have specifically asked you to do so. Imagine someone walking into your home, redecorating according to their taste and then calling up your place of work and handing in your resignation. When you ask them why, they tell you they did it because they love you and they know what's best for you. How do you feel? It's a beautiful thing to pray for others, but respect their autonomy and respect that they are, like you, on their own journey.

The way I offer prayers for my loved ones is always in this spirit unless I've been asked to pray for something specific. You can always ask people if they would like you to include them in your prayers.

⍢ If you have prayers for others now, with this in mind, set up a ritual space with the intention of feeling, embodying and offering your prayers for others. In micro, sense your love for that person. In medio, let that love shape you and become a dance. In macro, offer that prayer from your heart into the heart of the Great Spirit and let it go.

7. Take small steps

I've had to learn that the spirits in the imaginal world don't have the same concerns or challenges that we have in the physical world. In the spirit world, all time is now, all manifestation is instant, there's no need for rest and there's no physical body to look after. In bringing guidance and healing from the spirit world to the physical world, we need to learn to translate whatever we receive into small, everyday, consistent steps that move us in the direction of our dreams. If we don't, we are likely to overstretch ourselves and fail. Patience, discipline and consistency are the keys.

⍢ What vision or guidance have you received that you have been unable to manifest up until now? Can you break the steps to manifestation down into smaller steps? What small steps can you take now to deepen your relationship with the imaginal world and your dreams? How can you bring more awareness to the connection between what you dream and how your life is?

8. Enjoy the journey and celebrate results

In the process of making changes, improving ourselves and our lives and making our offerings, some things happen quickly and some don't. Some realizations that land in shamanic work take years to make their way into our lives. So it's important to be both committed and flexible. Just do your best to enjoy the journey as much as the destination.

   ✐ When you have success of any kind, it's important to notice it and celebrate it. What can you celebrate now? What can you give thanks for? What needs more attention?

9. Always pay attention to the basics

In each ritual we've done so far, I've asked you to take care to open and close the space properly. Whenever you open or complete a ritual, invoke or release all you've called and take some notes. Practise these basics until they become as natural and easy as riding a bike. I speak to my allies when I wake up, before I go to sleep, in the shower and, of course, in the preparation and in the work itself. The more I am aware of them, the more present I experience them to be.

Day 20: Integration

   ✐ On Day 20, your integration time, ask yourself and your guidance what you have learned and if there is anything from this enquiry you need support with. Are there things you need to reflect on? What steps do you need to take moving forward?'

Day 21: Dedication

   ✐ On Day 21, do a ritual to dedicate what you have learned to your ongoing progress and, of course, to all your relations.

❧❧❧❧

Congratulations. Each time you walk through these doors and back again, you discover a little more about the road you are on and strengthen the connection between the imaginal world and the physical world, between what you dream and how you live. Feet on the ground, head in the clouds, heart present. Right here. Right now. Your imaginary friends and your very real spirits at your side. Moving on. One step at a time, with an occasional quantum leap...

CHAPTER 11

Diamonds in the Dark

Responsibility, Retrieval and Renewal

*'There is no coming to consciousness without
pain. People will do anything, no matter how
absurd, to avoid facing their own soul. One does
not become enlightened by imagining figures
of light, but by making darkness conscious.'*

CARL JUNG

In reality, the door between the physical world and the imaginal
world is always open. Everything that we create on this Earth is a
dance between what we imagine and how we bring that vision into
form.

How we imagine the world to be is how we perceive it to be. The
Inner Shaman knows this and shamans the world over understand the
importance of freeing the imagination from old stories and meanings
that no longer serve us as individuals, communities or as a species. The

story that we are separate from each other and from nature still has a lot of momentum and power in our world. But as I travel, I see more and more people turning their imagination towards new possibilities. And it's an obvious thing to say, but once we realize we have a choice, then we do. Sometimes it's good fortune that wakes us up. And sometimes it's a shock that makes us reassess our priorities.

Either way, to bring about lasting change, we need life energy. So I'm going to share with you a powerful shamanic technique that will give you access to the energy locked in your past. It's called *the SEER Process*. 'Seer' is another word for 'shaman' and in this case 'SEER' stands for Systemic Essential Energy Retrieval. The practice has its roots in the Toltec recapitulation traditions of South America. The ancient seers of that tradition understood that the main reason we find it difficult to integrate new understandings, visions and ideas is because we're already using all of our available life energy to maintain who we think we are. It takes a lot of life energy to keep the mask of self in place. Being practical people, the Toltecs turned their attention to discovering a source of energy that wasn't being utilized. Their brilliant discovery was that there's a massive amount of energy in the events that shaped our sense of self. The more emotional charge those events have when we remember them, the more life energy is being used to keep them frozen in time. The Toltecs devised a methodology through which they could revisit each situation, release what didn't belong to them and reclaim the life energy that had been used to keep the event frozen. Recapitulating the past became the central way of gaining more energy in the present. The Toltecs were also able to retrieve aspects of themselves that had got lost or put to one side along the way, and in so doing to become more whole in themselves.

EMBRACING THE PAST

The Inner Shaman knows the importance of embracing the past. If we leave it unexamined, we are destined to repeat its mistakes. But if we summon up our courage and take responsibility for our inheritance, we can transform it into high-octane fuel for creating what we are dreaming now. In this way, our medicine – the combination of our transformed experience, our Unbroken essence and our allies – becomes strong.

Early in my shamanic journey, I discovered the link between my own inability to feel my emotions and say what was in my heart and the trauma of my ancestors in the concentration camps of the Second World War. The inhumanity of that hell on Earth froze their hearts into silent submission. I experienced their terror and it overwhelmed me like a tsunami. Over several years, I gathered my resources until I felt strong enough to visit Auschwitz and do my own soul retrieval work there. The results of that journey transformed my life on every level. I was able to feel again and, step by step, release the ancestral terror, fury and grief I had been carrying.

I believe that all of us, given support, can break the chains of the past. I've witnessed people from a huge variety of cultures and backgrounds, carrying all sorts of horrors and hurts, standing up with newfound dignity and saying: 'This suffering ends here. I refuse to carry this any longer. And I refuse to pass it on to others in my life or to the next generation.'

Tony, an apprentice, put it like this:

I first came across Movement Medicine when I was in prison. I'd been struggling with addiction for a long time, getting clean, picking up, getting clean and picking up again. Rachel Morris [a trained Movement Medicine teacher] brought the work to us once a week. It was hard at first. I'd only ever danced in clubs. I was in my head all the time. We all were, worrying about what other people were thinking. But I started to look forward to those sessions. For the first time in my life, even though I was in prison, I got a taste of freedom.

When I was released, I went to Devon for a 10-day workshop with Ya'Acov and Susannah called 'Initiation'. It was hard. The majority of participants were white, mostly women. Most of them weren't English either, so there was a language barrier. My head was playing games with me. I was thinking, They can't know a thing about me, a black guy. Maybe all they know about me is what they read on the front page of a newspaper. *I felt awkward, separate, not as good as them. But they went out of their way to welcome me, to include me. I had to close my eyes to get into it. But I started to relax and the work started to make sense to me. I started to feel it all in my body.*

On the third day, we were working with the relationship with Mother. I went into the room in the morning and there were all these photos of people's mums on the wall. I felt really emotional. My mum had died while I'd been in prison. I'd made amends with her before, but then I'd relapsed again and never got the chance to make it up to her. Ya'Acov was asking us to put ourselves in our mum's shoes, to imagine what life was like for her, the struggles she'd been through.

But it was the ancestor work that really got me. Especially because the room was full of white people. There went my head again, thinking, What do you guys know about pain? *But then I remembered,* I'm here to do my work. *And there it was: the colonial times. They were under the whip. They had no freedom of choice. They were separated from their families. All that abuse and all that rape!*

I could hear Ya'Acov saying, 'Let your body be like water. Water always finds a way through.' And then I was crying like I'd never cried before – floods of tears. I got that this was healing. Ya'Acov was saying, 'Stay on your feet, keep moving.' My legs were going, but three women came and held me up, two at my sides and one in front. We were in eye contact and suddenly I felt something I'd never felt before. People can say that they care or even act like they care. But at that moment, I felt cared for. I felt it.

Now, whenever I dance, my ancestors are there – my mum, my dad, my sister. I've felt my dad's pain – coming to the UK all alone to work, how his father treated him. And I've been able to understand him and forgive him. It's that healing energy – it helps me to feel what my ancestors felt. Just surviving from one day to the next. Under that whip. I feel their pain, but I'm not living it. When I dance their story, their oppression, it's a freedom dance. I've moved from feeling that oppression to knowing I'm protected. The dance puts me in a trance, out of my head, and I feel it.

My intuition has come alive now. I've started to see myself in a different light. My self-esteem has gone up. I don't always make the right choices, but this Inner Shaman, the wisdom, it's there all the time.

No matter how broken we may feel, as long as our heart is still beating we have it within us to rise up with the morning sun and use yesterday's disappointments and hurts as motivation to break free today. I love that about our species. And in the dream I'm dreaming, I see more and more people becoming aware of the value of facing the past. Though we can't change it, we certainly have it within us to change our relationship to it and update the meaning we have derived from it.

The SEER Process is an excellent and effective tool for transforming our relationship to the past. Quite simply, it works. And the result is a massive surge of creative energy in the present. Imagine for a moment what life would be like if you were no longer dragged down by the weight of your history, but fuelled by it.

SOUL LOSS AND SOUL RETRIEVAL

Of course, it's not just our ancestors' experiences that need our attention, but also our own. As children, we're like sponges: we soak up information in every way possible from the environment we're in. We're also brilliant survivors. When we're faced with intolerable situations, we have the capacity to disassociate from our physical body and escape to the imaginal realm. And just as the physical body is capable of isolating threats to its health and separating them off in order to ensure the best possible running of the system, the psyche is capable of doing the same. In the shamanic world, this separation is called *soul loss*. It doesn't sound good, but it is genuinely good news. By packing away aspects of ourselves, we keep them safe from harm. And when we find the support and internal strength to face, feel and release the pain of those experiences, we can reintegrate the parts that dissociated. That is *soul retrieval*.

It isn't always easy. The Inner Shaman knows that healing is possible, but healing sometimes means accepting that some wounds leave permanent scars and the best we can do is learn to live with them. At other times, healing means profound and even apparently miraculous transformation. In all cases, shamanic healing takes persistence and care. We need the safety and courage that the Dancing Warrior brings. We need the warm and clear presence of the Wounded Healer. We need the patience and love of the Wise Elder. And if we are to imagine doors where once there were just brick walls, we need the humour and creativity of the Dancing Fool. With all of these in place, I've been privileged to witness many people recovering from some of the worst kinds of trauma we can inflict on one another and becoming some of the most empowered and creative people I know.

Soul retrieval means returning to the past with all the allies and support we have now. We don't go back in order to re-experience what happened. It was bad enough the first time. We go back to change our relationship to it. Our Inner Shaman knows how to use the power of embodied imagination to do that. They acknowledge and release old emotions and create fertile empty space so they can retrieve our qualities of soul, our diamonds hidden in the dark. If you're reading these words, you've already more than survived whatever life has put in your path. If you are willing, your Inner Shaman can show you how to transform that past into medicine.

Many years ago, I was fortunate to meet an extraordinary medicine woman who was known by her students as Grandmother Thunder. She was Argentinian by birth and had spent her early teenage years in the notorious concentration camp known as Bergen-Belsen. I met her just two weeks before she died. Two of her students asked me if they could bring her as a guest to a Movement Medicine workshop I was teaching in Amsterdam. I was honoured to have her there. She sat in a chair at the side of the room and witnessed our work. She knew she was dying and had already made her peace with that. The reality of mortality and the grace of acceptance shone from her.

At the end of the day, we had a short conversation. Her students asked her to bless me, but she told them, much to my amusement, that I was already blessed enough. Instead, she had a request. She asked me if I would be willing to take half of her ashes to Israel and find a suitable place somewhere near Jerusalem to scatter them. I was touched and agreed at once.

Two months later, I was on a plane to Tel Aviv to run a five-day workshop and her ashes were in my backpack in a small jar wrapped in a beautiful silk scarf. By then, her students had told me a little more about her life. She'd experienced the trauma of seeing some of her family die in Bergen-Belsen. And, in some ways even worse, she'd seen how the people who survived often did so at the expense of their dignity and humanity. When she was liberated from the camp on 15 April 1945, at the tender age of 15, she'd pledged her life to healing. And she'd been clear from the beginning that any genuine healing had to include her relationship with the guards at the camp and the land and people of Germany.

When she was 70 years old, she'd taken part in a vision quest on land not far from Bergen-Belsen. She had been due to be out for 72 hours without company, food or water, but on the second morning the weather had taken a turn for the worse and the quest leaders had been worried about her. So they'd asked for a volunteer from the support team to go and check she was okay. A young German man stepped forward.

He was expected back within a few hours, but he didn't return that day or during the night. Eventually, at the end of the quest, he returned with Grandmother Thunder, arm in arm. It was clear to everyone who saw them that something significant had transpired between them.

It turned out that the young man's grandfather had been one of the guards at Bergen-Belsen. The young man had always carried a heavy burden of guilt about his family's Nazi past. But out on that mountain, just as Grandmother Thunder had intended, healing had taken place.

Grandmother Thunder worked tirelessly her whole life to connect with those who were supposed to be her enemies. She was one of those people who just refuse to believe in the 'us and them' story.

In Tel Aviv, there was a strong older woman called Rivkah on the workshop who had heard I was carrying Grandmother Thunder's ashes. She told me she was studying with a holy woman who lived in the desert. After the workshop, a few of us, including Rivkah, drove to Jerusalem to find a suitable place to spread the ashes; I realized I had no idea how we would find a good place, but Grandmother Thunder had been a powerful medicine woman and I felt certain that something would guide us. Then I remembered the holy woman.

Rivkah phoned her teacher and she agreed to help. The plan was to call her when we reached the outskirts of Jerusalem. When we arrived in the hills surrounding the city, we found a place to pull over and called. The holy woman asked us to be still while she meditated. We sat quietly for a few minutes, waiting in silence. Eventually, she told us she was ready to give us directions.

She hadn't asked us where we were and this was before the time of satnavs, but she gave us precise instructions and we followed them. When we ended up in a suburban area in the hills, it didn't look promising, but Rivkah told us we were nearly there and if we took the next left, we'd find a small forest that would be the perfect resting place for Grandmother Thunder's ashes.

It was like being in a dream. Sure enough, we discovered a little forest and walked into it, glad of the shade and the fresh scent of the trees. After a while, we found a small clearing with a large tree at the centre. It was a beautiful place. We sat there quietly, then began to drum and sing. The mood was celebratory.

After a while, the wind quietened, the birds fell silent and everything seemed to be paying attention. It was clearly time to scatter the ashes. As we did so, I felt the spirit of Grandmother Thunder was so happy that a part of her had come back home. There was a beautiful blend of sadness and joy in the air as we left.

We took a different path back to the car, and just as we left the trees behind, we spotted a small wooden bench with a plaque on it. To our amazement, the English words on it said: 'This forest was planted to commemorate the lives of all those who died at Bergen-Belsen concentration camp. May you all find peace.'

Like many others, Grandmother Thunder showed us the power of choice. She imagined a healing road and then walked that road her whole life, touching many others on the way. She did it. So can we. The moment we recognize that we can choose a better meaning to take from the past is the moment we stand up and take responsibility for our lives. We stop looking for someone or something to blame and use the power we have to heal.

As I mentioned earlier, the most powerful and effective way I know of transforming our relationship with the past and bringing a whole lot more soul into the present is *the SEER Process*.

🌿 PRACTICE: THE SEER PROCESS 🌿
(SYSTEMIC ESSENTIAL ENERGY RETRIEVAL)

The intention of this practice is to transform your relationship with events from your past, retrieve and welcome home aspects of your soul, and increase the life energy available to you.

Timing

This will take approximately an hour.

Preparation

To begin, please make a list of nine events from your past that still have an effect on you now. How will you know? When you think of them, you may feel an emotional charge or a contraction in your body. They may irritate you like a thorn in your foot. Or they may make you wish to turn away.

I usually suggest that when you are doing this process for the first time, you work with a relatively minor event. It is also useful to walk through the process once before you actually begin. I suggest you then work with the nine events one by one, again over a period of 21 days. After that, you'll have a pretty good idea of the effectiveness of the process and you can go on from there or just use it when you need to.

The process involves moving from the present into the past and back again. Whenever you are doing work with the past that may involve strong feelings, only go as far as you are able. If at any time things become too intense, just step back into the present, ground yourself, resource yourself and continue when you are ready. The key reality check is to stay in connection with your body and your present moment resources. If you lose that connection, you're probably trying to take too big a step. Slow down. Take a smaller one. The results will be better.

This is a personal healing process, not one for doing work on behalf of somebody else without their permission (for example, 'I am doing this so that my colleague will recognize the foolishness of their ways'). Nor do we do this to send the emotional energy we've been carrying to anyone else. We may need to express emotion 'at someone' in the past, but we're doing this to *release* our feelings, not to dump them on anyone in the present.

Imagine a big extractor fan above you and switch it on before you begin, so that whatever is released is taken back to its origins. This is important.

Practice

- Set up your space and do whatever you need to do to become present in body, heart and mind. Move, drum, sing and feel free to use any of the practices we've already covered. Repetitive drumming music will help. Connect to your Inner Shaman and their archetypal helpers, and invite all that supports and guides you into the space.

- Imagine that the space in front of you represents the future and the space behind you the past. To your right, imagine your Wise Elder witnessing your journey. To your left, imagine what I call *the storehouse of life energy*. I like to see this as a beautifully organized storage space in which all the life energy that is locked in the past sits in labelled boxes, waiting to be made available in the present. Once you have done your work in the past, you will turn to this imaginary place and call back the life energy and soul that have been bound up in whatever story you are working with. (Ten minutes.)

- Turn towards your Wise Elder and go and stand at their side. Describe the constellation, i.e., 'The dancer is in the centre of the circle, resourced and connected to their medicine. Behind them, to the left of where I am standing with the Wise Elder now, is the past. To the right of that, opposite me now, is the storehouse of life energy.'

The SEER process

✍ Take a short time to describe the story you are going to work with. Describe it in the third person, i.e., 'When she was 21, this is what happened...'

✍ Point out the storehouse of life energy.

✍ And finally, point out the future road in front of the dancer (now to your right) and set the intention that that future will be free from the negative effects of the past event as a result of this *SEER Process*. (Five minutes.)

✍ Return to the centre of your circle and make sure the dancer in you is awake and present. Connect with the four elements physically and energetically. Visualize an extractor fan above you and switch it on. Still in the centre, see if you can allow yourself to feel in your body the effect this story has on you now. Let it move, but keep your breathing steady. (Five minutes.)

✍ Prepare yourself to step back into the story, taking all your resources with you. Feel your ground. Feel the Earth. Feel the power of the Fire inside you.

✍ Take a deep breath and step back into the story, knowing you are there to lend your resources to it and bring movement to it. You can move, speak and express yourself freely on behalf of the you who experienced this. You aren't looking for emotion, but if it's there, give it movement and sound. Sometimes this process is very quiet. Sometimes it's very loud. Give yourself 90 seconds now to express yourself, then take a short pause to regather your resources. Give yourself another 30 seconds if you need it. (Three minutes.)

✍ Well done. Now call the healing presence of the Waters to flow through the landscape of this story. Let your body become as fluid as the Waters. Release your joints. Breathe and let the Waters wash slowly through you and through the whole scene, purifying as they go. (Two minutes.)

✍ The next step is *shaking medicine*. Let yourself shake from the inside out, like a butterfly in a cocoon, so that your whole system is able to shed the tight skin of this story. Take as long as you need. Shake softly, shake strongly. Trust your Inner Shaman to lead the way. (Two minutes or more.)

✍ Now step back into the present and take some time to feel the space you have created inside you. Breathe it in.

✍ And now turn towards the storehouse of life energy. Open your arms, your imagination and your heart and say out loud:

> *I am calling back all the life energy that has been locked inside this story, every time I have remembered it and felt its repercussions. I am calling back the quality of soul and the life energy that I have been separated from as a result of this story.*

✍ Call the power of the wind and the breath of life. Take a deep breath and imagine yourself being flooded with this returning energy and soul. Dance them into your bones, your muscles, your blood, your very cells. Visualize them. Own them. They are your life energy and soul and are now available to you. Circulate them through your system, breathing slowly and deeply. (Three minutes.)

✍ Turn back briefly towards the past and acknowledge this story as part of your past. You may feel differently towards it now. Acknowledge what is true. Remember, when you are dealing with more difficult experiences that may have been repeated many times in your life, you may have to take smaller steps in order to free yourself completely. (One minute.)

✍ Now turn 180 degrees to face your future. Find a simple incantation that distils the essence of this process. For instance, if you were working with a story in which you felt your creativity was dismissed or not received, your incantation might be something like: *'I am free to be creative and my creativity is well received.'* Embody it, feel it, give it energy. Repeat it out loud. (Two minutes.)

✍ Imagine yourself, at some point in the next seven days, taking a small step that is congruent with your incantation. This will help you to know that you are integrating this *SEER Process* into your day-to-day life. The simpler the step, the better. Step forward into that future and imagine yourself taking that simple step. For example, if your *SEER Process* has been about not speaking your truth, you might imagine yourself in a situation where in the past you would have silenced yourself and this time taking a deep breath and speaking up.

✍ Turn around, imagine the part of you that did this *SEER Process* and thank them. Acknowledge them for their work. Wink at them. Blow them a kiss. (One minute.)

✍ Step back into the centre and see your future self acknowledging you. In turn, acknowledge them. Wink, blow them a kiss, congratulate them. This simple practice builds a little imaginal bridge between the dream and the actualization of that dream and it's an important part of integrating your work. (One minute.)

✍ Turn to your Wise Elder, thank them and welcome them back into your heart.

✍ Thank and release all that you called.

✍ Write down your incantation and the future step associated with it.

✍ Look in the nearest mirror and smile!

✍ Then take some time to rest and receive the echo of your work.

Well done! Brilliant work. Now you've got it, use it. It works. And the more you do this, the more confident you will become in your Inner Shaman's ability to use the power of their embodied imagination in this way. Their intention is to face the truth they uncover and move past it to discover the rough diamonds in the dark caves of the past. With time and practice, we can polish those diamonds until they shine like stars in the night sky.

❦❦❦❦

We need light to be able to see in the dark. To be who we are, responsibly, we need all the strength and resources that the Inner Shaman brings. We need to deepen our connection to the Unbroken and our own unique medicine and to bring a more authentic Self into all our relationships. And that's exactly where we're going next. Let's take a leap into the Inner Shaman's guide to relationship.

CHAPTER 12

1 + 1 = 3

The Inner Shaman's Guide to Relationship

'You don't develop courage by being happy in your relationships every day. You develop it by surviving difficult times and challenging adversity.'

EPICURUS

The potential alchemy that the Inner Shaman brings to all their relationships is 1 + 1 = 3. Two embodied humans who are aware of themselves and able to expand that awareness to include each other will generate a creative and fertile space called *conscious relationship*. When both people care for that relationship as if it were a third entity, so much more becomes possible.

The Mesa Practice (p.69) is the Inner Shaman's way of learning how to stay aware of their own backbone as they expand their awareness to include another, and is the basis for more honest and clear one-to-one relationships of all kind. As we become more aware of our internal world through interoception, and as we strengthen our second skin through practice, our boundaries become clearer. And the clearer our boundaries are, the better prepared we are for the Inner Shaman's approach to relationship. Knowing our 'No!' is a prerequisite for knowing our 'Yes!' The more aware we are of ourselves, each other and the space between us, the clearer our communication and our capacity to see, be seen and be with the other.

I've heard it said many times that to be in a good relationship with another person, you have to be in a good relationship with yourself. While there is some truth in this, it's far from the whole truth. I've learned so much about how to be in a good relationship with myself from my long-term one-to-one relationships. I've learned that any relationship worth its salt will take us to our own edges and beyond, again and again. And despite our habit of complaining about the people who push our buttons, the Inner Shaman knows that if we want to find our power and put it to good use in this life, we have to take responsibility for the histories we bring with us into our relationships.

I've also heard it said that if life is a school, relationships are a university. For the Inner Shaman, relationships of all kinds carry the signature and brilliant precision of our old friend *the Great Choreographer*. I've noticed again and again how, with impeccable timing, life puts the people in front of me who deliver just what I need to become a little more conscious of who I am. Recognizing that our perception of other people is never accurate without interoception is a big step. If we know, when conflicts arise, that life is always trying to teach us more about who *we* are, then when we are triggered by another person, we'll know that the often painful emotions we're feeling are nobody's fault. They are signposts on the road to healing our broken heart. The pain we feel, though touched by what is happening in the present, is old.

It takes courage to take responsibility for our own experience. But when we do, we gain so much more clarity about how we are creating the continuous stream of disappointment, disillusion and conflict that is part of this territory.

Don't get me wrong – sometimes, even often, relationships are frustrating, unjust, unbalanced and unconscious. Sometimes we all need to let off steam and have a damn good moan about all those bastards who make our lives so complicated! However, there's a big difference between letting off steam and actually believing that someone else is to blame for our experience. Now, I'm not saying that we can't be wronged by another person. Clearly we can. But the Inner Shaman knows that freedom is rooted not in blame of self or other, but in responsibility. And responsibility means the willingness to ask ourselves, 'What is my part in creating this?'

When we are triggered or feel threatened, regardless of whether the perceived threat is real or not, we go into the fight-flight-freeze response, and in that state we are rendered incapable of seeing or hearing one another accurately. These triggers are inside us, and from the Inner Shaman's point of view, they get activated so that we can become aware of them and take responsibility for them. The deeper we travel, the more the Inner Shaman will help us to recognize the personal material and undigested experiences of our ancestors that we are carrying. These are ours to deal with, and though it may take time, if we do it, we will realize that none of us are without blame and none of us are without blood on our hands.

Taking responsibility for what arises inside us is a skill we need to learn and go on developing. And the sooner we start, the better. Admitting that we create our perception through the story we tell is a revolution. Having said that, I love it that there's always the chance that when we are present, wherever we look we'll see the Mystery smiling back at us, and the fortress around our heart will dissolve as if made of illusion.

In one-to-one relationships, the harvest of revealing our vulnerability and our power is a much deeper intimacy. Telling the truth, though scary at times, leads to more safety. In friendship, more intimacy leads to a much deeper understanding of ourselves, each other and the dynamics in the space between us. In sexual relationships, more intimacy leads to infinitely better sex, which is one of the most potentially healing and mutually empowering ceremonies I know. Now that's a harvest worth shovelling some shit for.

On the one hand, we are so simple. We want shelter, warmth and nourishment. We want to be safe from the threat of being attacked. We want good health. We want to be seen for who we are, and for the most part, we want peace. We want to be loved and we want to love. We want to be free to be ourselves and we want to learn. We want meaning that touches us and purpose that motivates us.

On the other hand, we are so complex. We hold on to our memories as if they were happening now. We hold on to our hurt as if it could replace the soul loss we're afraid we can't heal. We struggle with power. We fight with tight smiles on our faces, pretending that we're being so very reasonable while we're stabbing each other in the back with that sharp finger of blame. We hide our hurts behind our furies and deliver our revenge without shame, claiming that some god somewhere told us to. Maybe worst of all, we hide our fear of difference behind ignorant certainties about each other that blind us to the spark of divine intelligence right there in front of us, trying to remind us what this theatre piece is all about.

The number one rule for the Inner Shaman in one-to-one relationships is to take responsibility for our 50 per cent of any challenges that arise and do the work to discover the roots of those challenges within our own and our ancestors' histories.

FOUR RELATIONSHIP LENSES

Now that I've described the territory, let's get down to work. I'm going to invite you to ask your Inner Shaman to work with the past, present and potential future of your relationships through four different lenses:

- Family relationships

- Lover/partner relationships

- Friendships

- Power relationships

All of these four areas of one-to-one relationship present different challenges and different opportunities for the Inner Shaman to learn. It's quite likely that you'll feel stronger in one area than another. I suggest you allow yourself to be fascinated by both your apparent areas of strength and your apparent areas of weakness.

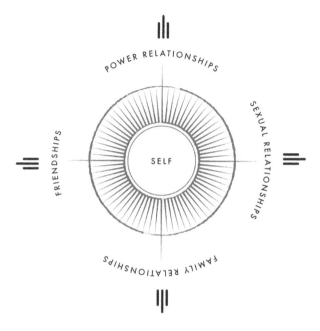

Relationships map

I invite you to put yourself at the centre of the circle. Doing so is indicative of your willingness to take responsibility for your part in any and all of the relationships in which you find yourself.

South: Family Relationships

There are those who say that the deepest part of our intelligence chooses the perfect family and environment for us to grow up in. And there are those who wonder if perhaps they were adopted, so different do they feel from their family of origin. Perhaps the truth lies somewhere in between. But a more interesting question might be: 'What needs healing from my experience of growing up in my family and culture, and how can I transform that experience into medicine so that I can become more responsible for myself and enhance the quality of all my one-to-one relationships?'

Recently, I had a conversation with a fellow shaman called Sergio Magaña about how long it had taken us to bring our medicine home to our family of origin. Both of us had taken the road less travelled and gone far beyond our family's expectations of how we should live our lives. We recognized what a challenge the choices we had made had been to our families. And we regretted the pain our choices had brought them. But we also knew that doing our best to heal those relationships was as important as any other work we might be doing elsewhere. We both knew we owed our existence to our ancestors and acknowledged the struggles they and our parents had gone through. We were amused and touched to realize that it had taken both of us 20 years to feel at ease enough in ourselves to really show up for our families with our medicine. And we both understood that sharing ours meant honouring theirs in a new way.

A few years ago, I received a simple instruction in a ceremony: 'Next time you go to your family home, take your medicine with you.'

It had taken my family many years to see the value of the life I had chosen. And in all honesty, I had my criticisms of them too. For many years, I felt that I couldn't bring my real self into the family for fear of being criticized and misunderstood. But recognizing that I was playing a full part in that dynamic by keeping separate and not recognizing my own criticisms really helped me to understand that it was within my power to change the dynamic.

Visiting family is always a good reality check. The status quo of the family system, whatever that is, depends on us all continuing to play our usual roles. Like a strong rip current, family systems have quite a pull. When I was with my family, I noticed that I was often acting as if I was a puppet being operated by invisible connections to the past, still acting as a child rather than an adult, waiting to be recognized and praised for who I had become.

The instruction I had received in ceremony had been an invitation from spirit to grow up and focus on what I could honour and praise in my family. And so I did. I went to see them, knowing that I had something to offer and I could choose to offer it freely, without concern about how it was received. That choice brought new life into the old system. We all seemed to open up to one another in a new way and our family table became a more heartful, listening and enjoyable place. I was surprised and delighted that such a simple choice could have such a positive result.

For many of us growing up in the industrial world, our family has been a source of trauma and has damaged our basic trust in others. But I have been privileged to witness many people healing their wounds and returning to their family homes with their heads held high. The result has often been genuine transformation in seemingly rigid family situations. For the Inner Shaman, healing is a necessity, not a luxury. 'The chain of suffering ends with me' is a very strong motivation and I want you to know that, as impossible as change may sometimes seem, with the help of your Inner Shaman, you are capable of creating a miracle.

East: Lover/Partner Relationships

The first thing to acknowledge here is that for the Inner Shaman, there's no such thing as casual sex. Once we open up to another human being in that way, it's like going from the first analogue internet connection to the fastest digital speed available in terms of the bandwidth of information that passes between us. That can be a wonderful thing and, as we all know, it can be quite the opposite.

As you now know, for the shaman, sexuality is the most potent and sacred gift we've been given. It is the elemental forces of life dancing through our physical body in a way that touches the very essence of our spirit. It has the power to create life and to literally make (as in manufacture) love. And I'm not just talking about babies. Making love is a ceremony in itself.

With intimacy, sexual ecstasy, and the profound spiritual and physical nourishment it brings, is much more possible. Intimacy means honesty. It means living without secrets and having an ongoing commitment to healing shame and feelings of inadequacy. I dream of a world in which we are taught to honour our sexuality, recognize its power and use it to enhance our lives and the lives of those we share it with.

In the modern world, long-term relationships in which both partners are committed to supporting each other in being truly themselves are rare. Even rarer are long-term relationships in which both partners recognize that genuine intimacy is the key to a sex life that actually gets better and better over time. I have been with Susannah for 33 years. In that time we've taught each other how to be the lover we'd always dreamed of. There's no way we could have done that without facing our shit together and going to the edge and back in many ways. Anyone who tells you that a long-term relationship is easy hasn't been in one. If we are with anyone for long enough, everything that might come between us and our capacity to love will show up. And the edge is never far away. I don't know of any long-term relationships that haven't been to that edge and very nearly fallen off it, my own included.

In 1998, Susannah and I were living in a five-storey house in Nottingham. We had moved there to work out if there was life in an unconventional form of relationship we were discovering, which was triangular in nature. We all learned a lot until it became untenable for many reasons and the third party graciously stepped out. What followed was the hardest time in our married life. We really didn't know how or if to find each other again.

One day, we were sitting on high stools at the breakfast bar. The kitchen floor was red quarry tiles which we'd polished back almost to their original best. We were drinking wine out of a pair of Dartington crystal glasses that we'd been given for our marriage in 1989 and we were having the same frustrating conversation that we'd been having for several months. We were completely stuck between a rock and a hard place and at our wits' end.

At one point, I held my empty wine glass out over the edge of the breakfast bar and said to Susannah: 'This is our relationship.'

I then let the glass fall, fully expecting it to shatter on the hard surface. What actually happened was one of those pearl moments in my life that I carry in a little pouch hidden inside me. I hope to have the time just before I die to take those pearls out one by one and offer them back to life with my full gratitude for their artistry and beauty. That day I watched as the world went into slow motion, that well-known state that accompanies moments when death is present. The long-stemmed glass hit the floor and bounced twice on its side before settling into place, fully upright and totally unharmed.

I literally gasped in shock. And I knew right then that the conversation was over. The vows I had made on our wedding day had faced the storm and stood firm. I picked up my drum there and then to sing for and thank whichever helping spirits had caught that glass and steadied it and us in the same heartbeat.

That wasn't the end of our challenges, but it was the beginning of a new chapter. Step by step, we travelled through the tricky terrain of unacknowledged hurts and betrayals that had led us to that edge.

Each time we find the courage to track the original pain from our childhood or from our ancestral line that has found its way into the space between us, intimacy grows and making love lives up to its name.

West: Friendships

Friendship runs through life like a river, keeping the landscape alive and fluid. Good friendships help to keep us afloat when storms come. As time has marched on, my good friends have become more important to me. The further I have travelled, the more I have recognized just how important honest, loving friendships are to anyone who dares to wield power in this world. And whenever we take new steps on our journey, we need friends to acknowledge us, keep our feet on the ground and help us to fly.

If we are to be successful in pursuing our dreams and becoming who we are, we need to ensure that we have people around us who are unafraid to challenge us and delighted to laugh at us and with us when we trip up along the way. The only thing that is certain is that we will.

Real friendship involves sacrifice. But when we give ourselves wholeheartedly when our friends are in need, unexpected teachings and rewards come to us. Many years ago, I was in a ceremony being held in a large and freezing cold marquee in Belgium. The stove wasn't working and rain was falling outside. We were there with a dear friend who was going through a torrid health challenge. The makeshift toilets were outside and at one point I noticed that he had been gone a while. I got my coat on and went outside to look for him. I found him stuck in the loo in some discomfort. I stayed with him for a while, getting colder and wetter by the minute, until one of the shaman's assistants showed up and said he could take over. I was so relieved to hand my friend over and go back inside. I quickly took off my wet clothes and got inside my sleeping bag to try and warm up.

I was just getting comfortable and getting into my own journey when I heard the quiet yet insistent voice of my Inner Shaman asking me, 'Ya'Acov, what does friendship mean to you?'

I resisted as long as I could, but I knew I couldn't stay in the now cosy warmth of my own cocoon. Eventually, feeling miserable, I extricated myself, put my cold, wet clothes back on and went outside again. My friend was still in pain, so I stayed with him, singing and praying in the rain. There was one moment of relief when the humour of the situation burst through and we laughed so hard that I got warm and his pain eased. Finally the rain ceased and he was ready to exit the toilet. The organizers had lit a fire outside and we sat as close to it as we could to dry out. I felt so bedraggled and wet, yet good, whole and peaceful sitting with my friend by the fire under the clearing skies. Sometimes, the strongest healing is to simply surrender and be at a friend's side.

Like fine wine, friendships mature. None escape moments of conflict, misunderstanding or disagreement. If we stay around another person long enough, we're going to get to know their gremlins as well as their luminosity. Just as they'll know ours. An old shaman once told me that the challenges that life places on our road are the stones against which we sharpen the blade of our intent. Challenges in friendships are the same.

And sooner or later Death will come into the room and remind us that our time here is relatively short and there'll be no time left to settle for second best in ourselves, another person or the space between us.

North: Power Relationships

Power relationships are relationships where there is an inbuilt power differential between us and the other person: for example, teacher and student, boss and employee or parent and child. From the very moment we are conceived, we all experience the immense vulnerability that is part of these relationships. As children, our mother, father and the community we are born into hold the power of life and death over us. And the structures we inherit from the families, cultures and histories we are born into form the unconscious ground of our challenges in one-to-one power relationships.

There's no denying there are colossal imbalances of power in the world and there have been, and continue to be, huge injustices in historical and socio-political power relationships. They are part of the ground we walk on and have an effect on the power dynamics between us. There's also no denying we have inflicted massive hurts on one another. I want to encourage you to look at how you are in your power relationships and take it as an invitation from your Inner Shaman to create something new.

Once you've invoked the Inner Shaman, it's a fair bet to say that they might just team up with that quiet voice of conscience inside you. Every time you step back into the shadow dance and insist on playing another episode of the Victim–Persecutor–Rescuer–Hungry Ghost series (*After all, if there's a problem, it has to be somebody's fault*), you might just hear that little voice reminding you that every situation (*Yes! Every situation!*) is an opportunity to practise. Practise what? Remembering your resources. Recognizing that how you are perceiving the world probably isn't how the world actually is. Showing up honestly, with integrity. Recognizing the power you do have, taking responsibility for your part in creating any situation you are in and learning the maximum you can from it.

If we do continue to claim to be the casualties of everyone else's bad behaviour while paying little or no attention to our own, liberation will elude us and sticks, stones and damning judgements of all kinds will continue to polarize us. It's time to get real about and take responsibility for the underlying hurts we *all* feel. I strongly believe that the Inner Shaman's direct connection to the one kind of power that nobody can give or take from us – the personal power of a human being who knows who they are – is both the way through and the way out. My friend Jake often reminds me that the most dangerous thing we can do with our power is to deny it. As we become empowered through our work, we need to acknowledge our power and constantly update our picture of ourselves to avoid falling back into old habits.

It seems to me that we are living through the adolescence of our species. We have learned a lot. If we are to learn more, we need to grow up and dream a new dream. I know we can. We just need a few things. We need courage and mercy in equal measure. We need to create safe spaces where we can release the trauma from our collective unconsciousness about power relationships of all kinds. We need to know that our experiences and our feelings are going to be heard. We need to go beyond political and historical rights and wrongs. Like it or not, we are all family here. No exceptions. Choice by choice and action by action, every one of us is deciding how this human drama will unfold.

Remember the alchemical blend that the Inner Shaman is looking for in all their one-to-one relationships: 1 + 1 = 3. It's time to bring this enquiry into the powerful container of ritual space. We're going to cross the *arc of time* to learn from the past, acknowledge the present and create an up-to-date vision for the evolving future of all our relationships.

 PRACTICE: 1 + 1 = 3 – CREATING YOUR PERSONAL VISION FOR RELATIONSHIP

Timing

You will need one hour for this practice.

Preparation

- Set up your space in the normal way and then create three signs: 'Past', 'Present' and 'Future'. To begin with, place them in the South, the direction of family relationships.

✍ Once again, do whatever you need to do to become present in body, heart and mind. Move, drum, sing and feel free to use any of the previous practices. Music with a repetitive rhythm will help. Connect to your Inner Shaman and their archetypal helpers and invite all that supports and guides you into the space.

Practice

South: Family relationships

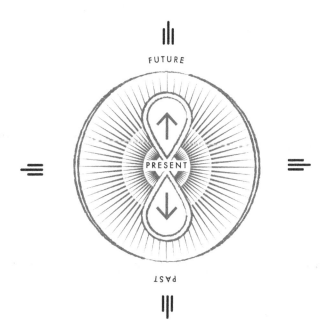

Past, present and future relationships

✍ Once you feel present, step into the South of your circle with the clear intention of working with the family dynamics in which you learned about relationships. Begin in the centre in the present. Ask your Inner Shaman to describe through your movement and through words the current condition of your one-to-one relationships with your family. Enquire as honestly as you can, using all the skills you have practised so far to embody what is true.

✐ Now, sense the arc of time that stretches from behind you, from your past with your family and the past of your family, all the way to the space in front of you, to your future and that of your descendants (even if you have no children yourself).

✐ Step back into the past, taking with you all the resources you have now. You're looking for the root experiences that shaped your family relationships and still affect all your one-to-ones. This is basically a fact-finding mission, so just make a note of what you find, especially any specific incidents that still have an emotional charge for you. These are all good stories to work through at some later point with *the SEER Process* (p.185). For now, if emotions arise, simply allow them to move.

✐ Okay, good. Once you've finished, step back into the present and do whatever you need to do to resource yourself.

✐ Look into the space ahead of you, the road to your future. How might you develop these relationships as you move forward? Consider this from the present.

✐ When you are ready, step firmly forward into your future and pay careful attention to what arises in your body, your feelings and your imaginal space. The future is uncertain, but the Inner Shaman is more than capable of receiving new information that can help you to 'dream in' the best possible outcomes for all your one-to-one family relationships. As always, only focus on your own behaviour, on what you are responsible for. Don't imagine the changes that you think others should make. Those are up to them and not your business. Take whatever time you need here.

✐ Once you are ready, step back into the present. Take a moment to digest what you have learned and resource yourself again.

East, West and North: Sexual relationships, friendships and power relationships

🖎 Now repeat the process in the East with your sexual relationships, the West with your friendships and the North with your power relationships. Whenever you step into the past, remember that you are there to witness the work that needs to be done. Gather the information from each direction so that you have a list of juicy events for your *SEER Process* work.

Centre: Evaluation

🖎 Once you have finished, spend some time back at the centre of the circle, digesting what you have learned. See all these different types of relationships around you and ask yourself:

~ 'What would help me most to take responsibility for myself in all my relationships?'

~ 'What needs to change inside me so that my relationships will realize their potential?'

~ 'What does the alchemy of 1 + 1 = 3 look like for me?'

~ 'What do I wish to give in my friendships, partnerships and other relationships?'

~ 'What do I wish to receive?'

~ 'Who do I need to become to give and receive this?'

~ 'What really matters to me in my relationships?'

~ 'What kind of a family member/lover/friend can I mature into and how can I develop responsibility in my power relationships?'

✍ Take some time to write down all the events from the past that showed up and design a plan to take them one by one through *the SEER Process* (p.185).

✍ Then complete your ritual in the normal way, making sure to leave enough time for the echo.

❧❧❧❧

I think George Bernard Shaw was channelling his Inner Shaman when he reminded us that it's up to us whether we choose to be 'a force of nature instead of a feverish little clod of ailments and grievances, complaining that the world will not devote itself to making us happy'.

This work with responsibility in relationships is an ongoing and fascinating journey. You now have your Inner Shaman's help as you move forward. Let's see how they can help you now, as you focus on the profound and urgent task of taking your place in relationship with the wider community of life of which we are all part.

CHAPTER 13

It's All about We

Changing the Dream
of the Modern World

*'Hope is not the conviction that something will
turn out well but the certainty that something
makes sense, regardless of how it turns out.'*

VACLAV HAVEL

A ugustin Tentets, a young Achuar warrior, stood before us in his full traditional dress: a bright red, yellow and black toucan feather head-dress and a cloth sarong. He held his spear as he spoke. The Achuar are an undefeated people who have made the choice to end the fighting between themselves in order to turn their collective strength towards protecting the Amazon rainforest in which they live from a common enemy – what they call *the dream of the modern world*.

Augustin told us that his great-grandparents had seen this time coming and that despite the strong forces stacked against it, the forest would stand. It would stand because of the alliances they and their neighbours would make with people like us from the outside world. He held his spear upright as he told us about the Eagle–Condor prophecy that says humanity will evolve by bringing together the knowledge and understanding of all cultures and learning to work together. He looked right at us then and told us that every one of his people – men, women and children – would go to the grave to protect their home. He showed us his warrior's heart, the strength of a person who will do whatever they need to do to protect life. No one doubted that he was speaking the truth.

Afterwards, Jorge, an Achuar elder in a wheelchair, rolled himself forward. He spoke in a much softer voice about why the oil had to stay in the ground for the health of the forest, its people and all peoples. He told us that his great-grandchildren would continue to live healthy lives on their ancestral lands because of our alliance. By welcoming us as guests and recognizing us as people with something to offer, he and his people reminded us that we were one family, sharing one biosphere and one destiny.

The shaman's knowledge is direct. It's not written in a holy book, it's written in nature. Nature tells shamans about the crisis we are facing. Nature tells everyone. But too many of us aren't yet listening. The Shaman in you is listening. They aren't caught in the storm of distraction that has descended on the modern mind. They know we're all one family living on one Earth under one sky. And what we do to one another and to our environment, we do to ourselves.

The facts of our current crisis are increasingly hard to bear. As I'm writing today, the rainforest in Brazil is burning. A part of me wants to conjure up that binary beast of blame and counter-blame and point my finger at President Bolsonaro. But he and the many others like him are just manifestations of the story we've been telling for a long time: the story that the Earth is just a resource for us to use as we please. And whilst it's important to stand up for what we believe in, simply standing on our soapboxes and making others the bad guys is no more than the same old road to a war in which we all lose.

Faced with the constant and overwhelming stream of bad news about what we've done, what we're doing and where this is all likely to end up if we don't change fast, it's not surprising that so many of us feel overwhelmed and hopeless. I hear many people asking, 'What difference will recycling make when the ice caps are melting?'

It's true that we've brought irreparable harm to the land, to the many species that are becoming extinct every day and to one another. But we've also created an extraordinary imperative to change: our very survival. And from a shamanic perspective, we know everything is connected and everything matters. We're not powerless. If we choose to live according to what's true for us, we'll be more effective and feel more fulfilled. If we stay connected to the power of nature, we'll be so much more resilient. And when we're more resilient, we'll be more creative and more connected to the love for life that is beneath despair.

So, if your heart is still beating, don't give up. Instead, I urge you to become one of the millions of people from all walks of life who are waking up to the urgency of this task. Waking up means embracing the reality of our situation and finding out who we actually are and what is ours to do. And there is nothing more fulfilling in this world than working every day to create something of beauty that dignifies our humanity and that we can pass on to future generations. You can invite your Inner Shaman to help you and become part of the solution. You can ask them to show you how to dream a dream that inspires you, and live in a way that is guided by that vision.

The alternative is more of the same. When we lose hope, our will and strength slip away. And when we lose our will, our unexpressed fury becomes hate and blame and our unexpressed grief solidifies into depression. We enter survival mode, our Hungry Ghosts take over and we do what we can to block the pain. Those Hungry Ghosts are rooted in our collective choice to numb our pain rather than face it and heal. It's a bizarre paradox that these days we're much more likely to die of overeating than of starvation. Addictions and distractions come in every shape and size, and they're all on sale. If we buy now, we can have two for the price of one and they'll both be here in the morning. But before we know it, we'll be locked into the vicious circle that keeps us heading at full speed towards any number of catastrophic visions of the future.

No! The Shaman in me will *not* accept that. I know and feel both the magnificent beauty and the heart-aching pain of the world. I hear the roars of the jaguars and see the silent tears of the burning trees. The Shaman will never turn away. They can't. They are compelled to stand up and dance so they can find the courage to be alongside their family. Dancing with the pain of the world is no bad thing. It doesn't lead to depression, but reminds us how much we love. If a dear friend were dying, would you turn away or do your best to bring as much beauty and love to them while they were still alive?

Love – not the kind that smothers suffering with sickly sweetness, but the real thing, perfume, petals and thorns – is the greatest motivational force in this universe. So, when feelings of despair enter my heart, I drum to settle my mind until it clears. I drum to feel the rhythm of life inside me until my body is awake and moving as it was designed to do. I dance to hear what my heart knows. I dance to feel the power of Earth, Fire, Water and Wind moving through me, restoring me to myself. I dance and I let the fury open me until the Waters of my heart can move again and I can grieve for what we have done to one another and to our beautiful planet. It is grief that opens the door to the vast storehouse of love that the Inner Shaman has for this life.

And so I dance through the heartache to reach beyond myself. I dance through whatever my heart feels. I acknowledge it, feel it and let it go. And I keep moving until I've let go of everything. And as I do so, I expand and I am touched by the force that this whole universe exploded out of nearly 14 billion years ago. I feel the presence of what I experience as the shining black light of peace of my Creator flooding through me and I am back in the Great Mystery. This is my oasis and here I am renewed again. I remember that the intelligence that is life evolving through everything goes far beyond what we have even begun to understand. And I find the strength to return.

As I do so, I know who I am and I know what matters to me. I know that if I spend too much time worrying about the outcome, I'll just sit down and give up. The future is always unknown. I have to accept that. What I keep coming back to is the urgency I feel to play my part in doing what indigenous peoples the world over are telling us we need to do: change the dream of the modern world. The clearly defined intention of that dream is individual identity and personal happiness. We are told we can consume our way to happiness and so we try to. But our consumer culture is really a futile attempt at self-medication and it doesn't work. It destroys the dignity of the soul and it's destroying the Earth too. What we really need is to heal the trauma that is driving us. And we need a new dream, a vision that recognizes that we belong to this world rather than it belonging to us.

When I first went to the Amazon, I remember clearly how worried and upset I was about the state of our planet. In ceremony, I asked the spirits of the forest to help me and show me how to make the best contribution to changing and improving the world. I was given a vision of two magnificent horses racing neck and neck towards a finishing line that was always moving further and further away. One was called Destruction and the other Creation. They were playing their roles to perfection. At times, it looked like a fight between two forces; at other times, I saw how the interplay between them created the high drama of evolution, the blend of agony and ecstasy that is life on Earth. I saw an adolescent species with an adolescent rationale. I saw extraordinary greed and extraordinary kindness. I saw our freedom to choose and the connection between our choices and the outcome we are living. And I saw us hungering for a new dream but so often feeding ancient Hungry Ghosts instead.

What I was shown put the Fire of hope and the passion to act in me. I had a vision of the beginning of time. I was shown how everything came out of nothing. I was shown the evolution of the universe and how it experiences itself through me, through you and through everything. I was shown the massive force of the Earth and of nature and its extraordinary ability to adapt. And I was told in no uncertain terms that though my worries about the health of the planet were well-founded, I should be much more immediately concerned about the health and wellbeing of my own species. And of course, I was told to begin with myself.

The Inner Shaman knows that our actions today will have a strong effect on what happens tomorrow. We are a truly remarkable species, capable of extraordinary achievements on every level. But the collective story that we are separate from one another and from nature is what is driving us now. We need to tell a new story based on the old shamanic knowledge that we *are* nature and the modern scientific understanding that *everything* is interconnected.

In 2015, the United Nations created the *2030 Agenda for Sustainable Development*. It's based on the five 'P's: People, Planet, Prosperity, Peace and Partnership. I've included a shortened version of it here because it's such an inspiring, mature and global vision for our collective future:

People
We are determined to end poverty and hunger, and to ensure that all human beings can fulfil their potential in dignity and equality and in a healthy environment.

Planet
We are determined to protect the planet from degradation, including through sustainable consumption and production, so that it can support the needs of present and future generations.

Prosperity
We are determined to ensure that all human beings can enjoy prosperous and fulfilling lives and that economic, social and technological progress occurs in harmony with nature.

Peace
We are determined to foster peaceful, just and inclusive societies which are free from fear and violence.

> **Partnership**
> We are determined to implement this Agenda through a
> revitalised Global Partnership for Sustainable Development,
> based on a spirit of strengthened global solidarity.
>
> ...If we realize our ambitions across the full extent of the
> Agenda, the lives of all will be profoundly improved
> and our world will be transformed for the better.

Wow! That this document exists is remarkable in itself. Whether we can implement the Agenda is down to the millions of micro-choices that each and every one of us makes every day.

Reading the United Nations Agenda has showed me that the imagination is there. And just like every impossible dream that ever was, we have to see beyond what may be possible. That is the joy of living life to the full, guided by a strong vision that makes absolute sense to us, regardless of the outcome.

Having said that, it's time to put the Inner Shaman back to work to help you to craft your own personal vision for the future. Bearing in mind that a good vision is always a masterpiece in progress, let's go for a shining diamond of a vision. Diamonds are created under enormous pressure and we have no shortage of that. I'm going to invite you to pray for a vision that has the ability to make you smile when you wake up in the morning, a vision that gives context to your choices, brings you medicine and resilience and supports you in facing the challenges we all face as part of the community of life on Earth. And I'm going to invite you to do that with as much joy, creativity and fulfilment as possible.

Anyone who has been successful at manifesting a dream will tell you that a good vision for the future is an excellent instruction manual for the present. If we know what we're trying to create, we can take small steps (with the occasional quantum leap) in the direction of that dream every day. E.F. Schumacher's 'Think globally, act locally' comes to mind.

A good vision comes from the deepest place of connection we can find between ourselves, our guiding spirits and the Great Mystery. It embraces the best possible outcome for ourselves, our relationships, our local community and the wider community of life. It includes our ancestors and is particularly aware of our responsibility to our descendants. Finally, the Inner Shaman can help you to discover a vision for life that is grounded in the power of love.

It's time now to ask your Inner Shaman to create a ritual space in which you can learn more about the art of both holding a vision for the future and, by connecting the macro vision to the micro details, in small everyday ways, live it now.

Though the airwaves are full of apocalyptic visions of the future and you may have many fears, I'm going to invite you to see beyond them and step into a future in which the United Nations Agenda has been successful and the world is telling a new story rooted in sustainability, justice and fulfilment for all.

🌿 PRACTICE: IT'S ALL ABOUT WE 🌿
– CREATING THE FUTURE NOW

Part of this ritual (from * to *) has been inspired by the wonderful work of Joanna Macy, an extraordinary environmental activist and Buddhist scholar.

Timing
You'll need one hour for this ritual.

Preparation
Set up your space quietly, focusing on praying for a vision. If you have the chance to do this ritual outside in nature, that would be excellent. If not, bring something from nature into your workspace to represent the wider community of life. Dedicating your work by saying 'For all my relations' is particularly significant in a ritual like this, in which you are seeking a vision that will help you to act on behalf of the wider community of life in these crucial times.

🖋 Put on music or work with a rattle or a drum if you have one. Start by *Awakening the Dancer* (p.29) and becoming present in body, heart and mind. Move, drum, sing and use any of the previous practices. Be sure to include *the Tree of Life* (p.57) and connect to the roots and the trunk so that your imagination can fly with your feet firmly on the ground. Connect to your Inner Shaman and invite all that supports and guides you into the space. Take the time to acknowledge the four directions, the elements and all your allies.

🖋 Make sure your body is warm and your joints are mobile.

Practice
🖋 Let's start with where you are in terms of the challenges we face as a species. How do they affect you? What are you already

contributing to your community, either locally or further afield? Take time to acknowledge your condition in both movement and words and celebrate how you are already part of the solution through your being and through what you are already doing. Work with Earth to become as grounded and as present as you can.

✐ Good. Now work with Fire and express what's in your heart in terms of your relationship to the wider web of life. Thank the Fire inside you and the light of the sun and ask the Fire to illuminate and help you express all that you feel about what's going on. Don't censor yourself. If you feel afraid, angry or just plain numbed out, invite the Inner Shaman to work with the dancer in you to find the shape and expression of what you feel. Don't hurry. Don't force it. Just give your beautiful animal heart the space to show you what it feels and how it moves.

✐ Now thank the Waters of life, inside and out, and ask them to help you release whatever you are carrying. Imagine a strong and healthy river running through you, washing your bones, your muscles, your blood and emptying your mind of all worries and doubts. Fall off the edge of yourself like a waterfall into a deep pool. Shake yourself free from distractions, become as fluid and as fresh as the Waters of life and then imagine yourself as an empty chalice, a hollow bone, ready to be filled to the brim with fresh vision.

✐ Well done. Now give thanks to the Wind and ask the Air to lift your mind into the sky. Take a little ride on the back of a beautiful broad-winged eagle. The view is spectacular. Fly with the eagle up into the empty blue sky and the shimmering light of the Upper World. Soar. Breathe in the Wind. Let it rush through you. Imagine it is clearing the fog of your daily affairs from around your body and blowing cool Air through the chambers of your heart, leaving the clear scent of freshness in its wake. Draw in that scent. Imagine the Wind's cooling spirit clearing your eyes, your throat, your head and your thoughts. Breathe deeply. Then let everything become still.

🖋 Imagine that your Inner Shaman is looking out from this clear space through the eyes of your heart. You are high enough now to see our blue-green planet on the outer edge of a galaxy in an unimaginably vast universe. Miracle or mystery, it's awesome. Imagine you can embrace the whole Earth from up here and let the Inner Shaman show you the tapestry of life on the planet. Look down on your own life and your relationship to the wider web of life. What do you see? Take some time to gaze down on it all, while you keep breathing and moving.

🖋 (*) Once you feel ready, you're going to move forward in time, year by year, then decade by decade, until you find yourself looking down on life on Earth 100 years from now. Be brave. Don't let anything distract you. Just keep your body moving to the rhythm. The rhythm and your movement are the fuel that feeds your capacity to dream. Look down on this future Earth now and take in the wonderful changes that have come to pass.

🖋 After a short while, you hear the voices of the children of the future and feel drawn to go down from the Upper World into their world. They greet you very warmly as their ancestors and you realize that they are your descendants. Take the time to witness their world and ask them any questions you have, while still keeping your body moving.

🖋 The children tell you that they've heard stories about your time. They say it must have been hard to live with such uncertainty about the climate and so much more. You tell them about life in our world and they thank you, with tears in their eyes, for what you did to make their world a possibility.

🖋 As you leave, they hand you a small gift, which you take in the palm of your hand, and ask you to come and visit them again. Your awareness returns to the Upper World and you look down once again on this future world, knowing that you will soon return to your own time and that you can come back here anytime. (*)

✐ Gazing down on the planet while journeying back through time is an opportunity to witness your own life. As you travel back now, with all that supports you close by, witness your own death and send a blessing. Don't dwell on it – the most important aspect of this journey is to discover more about how to live. So, as you travel back through the years of your life from the point of your death to the present, witness the choices that you make and the ways in which you choose to live.

✐ Again, be brave. Find a balance of kindness and determination as you witness your life. Leave perfection to the Creator. The best you can do is to live a life that is congruent with who you are and what matters to you. As you travel from the future towards the present, look carefully and honestly for any changes, both minor and major, that have been necessary for you to do that fully. Nothing is too small to matter and major changes can be broken down into manageable steps to be taken one at a time. Witness how you learned to live with more awareness of and connection to the web of life.

✐ Arriving back in the present, take a moment to feel that cool wind again. Before you return to Earth, gaze down on it and enjoy the mystery of it all. It's a beautiful planet. Wouldn't it be good for our species to mature? And for you to play your part in that?

✐ It's time to return to the present now, bringing your vision and gift from the future. Let your travelling spirit drop right back down into your body, then open your eyes and look around you. Affirm that you are fully back in your body and let it come to rest. Drink a glass of water and take some time to write down your vision of the future. Contemplate what it means for your life now and how you can contribute to bringing it into being.

✐ To help bring your vision to Earth, answer these questions:

～ 'What support do I need in order to ground what I have seen so that I can know myself as a unique and valued part of this human family and the wider community of life on Earth?'

~ 'What three things do I need to change in the next three months that will give me the peace of living congruently with what matters to me?'

~ 'What steps can I take in the next week that will water the seeds of this vision?'

Remember, small everyday steps work best – with the occasional quantum leap! If you saw yourself growing your own food, for example, but you don't have a garden, you could begin by growing some food in a window box.

✍ Complete your ritual in the normal way, making sure to leave enough time for the echo so that the effects of this powerful journey can land in the very cells of your being.

¥¥¥¥

My compliments once again to you. Another bold step taken! I'm singing your praises to the four winds and I see the children of the future thanking you for being part of changing the dream of the modern world, facing the unknown and dreaming a dream worthy of who you are.

Now you've dreamed it, please join me as we enter the last part of this book. It's time to bring in the harvest.

PART IV

HARVEST

*Partnering with the Source
and Serving Life*

'I saw the angel in the marble and carved until I set him free.'

MICHELANGELO

We've already been on quite a shamanic journey together. We started by building the foundations for encountering the Inner Shaman. We then empowered them through practice. And we undertook a deep enquiry into how they could help us take responsibility for that power. We worked to build a strong bridge between the imaginal world and the physical world and to recognize the ways in which we are the masters of our own perception through the stories we tell.

I'm sure you've noticed that relationship has been at the heart of our work. In all the rituals we do in our work, we include all of what we call *the Five Dimensions of Relationship*. We've already worked with the first four. We've deepened our relationship with ourselves (First Dimension), with others (Second Dimension), with the community of life (Third Dimension) and with the imaginal world (Fourth Dimension). The Fifth Dimension of relationship is the one that encompasses all the previous four: the Inner Shaman's relationship with the Great Mystery, God, the Creator. Deepening this relationship is the focus now. Welcome to the harvest!

You already know that shamanic practice isn't rooted in belief, but in direct experience that can be validated and put into context by our guides, both human and imaginal. So I won't be asking you to believe in anything. As always, I will be asking you to take the time to find out what is true for you and go on deepening your enquiry through the ongoing cycle of encounter, empowerment, responsibility and now harvest. This whole journey is structured to allow you to be guided by your Inner Shaman as you come closer to your own nature and to the great teacher that is nature itself. I once told a long-term apprentice that you couldn't learn shamanism from a book. (The Great Spirit clearly has a sense of humour!) It's true. Whatever you learn through these pages and through your embodied practice, at some point, to go deeper, you must take your practice out into the wild.

Nature is the great mirror because when we humans allow it to follow its course, everything in it is simply itself. Can you imagine the liberation and the joy you would experience if you, too, could learn to trust yourself enough to be who you are?

From a shamanic perspective, nature is the intelligence of the Great Spirit in physical form. It is the marriage of matter and spirit. Your body is made from the same material and animated by the same intelligence. When you reclaim that territory as your own, as you have been doing on our journey so far, then your spirit and all that it dreams can land firmly on this Earth and give what it came here to give.

All shamans who have chosen to serve life do so by partnering with the source. They understand that dreams that serve life grow in accordance with the seasons and the cycles of life and that their own journey through life is one such cycle. So in this next stage of our journey, we will look into how you can go on developing the abilities and skills of your Inner Shaman through looking at your life as an initiatory journey.

You will learn more about how you can enhance your experience of the present through changing the meaning you have taken from the past. You will have the chance to harvest more medicine and personal allies from the events that have made you who you are. Moving forward, we will also look at the future as a canvas on which to map the path to fulfilling your Inner Shaman's potential in this lifetime.

The last two chapters will bring in the harvest of our work, as we look more deeply into the Inner Shaman's relationship with the divine and invite them to leap into the embrace of the Great Mystery. For me, that place is a refuge. It is the still point in the storm of life where I can let everything go, even myself, and let God. Yes, I know – God is a really tricky word with a really tricky history. I didn't use it for decades because so many of the ways it had been used were in direct opposition to everything I stood for. But recently I've felt a strong need to reclaim the word, so sometimes I do. It makes my ancestors happy and it has power.

I very much appreciate the magnificent variety of religious and spiritual traditions that we have created, and the care, community, comfort and direct experience of the divine they have brought to so many. Sadly, fundamentalists of every description continue to pursue the mistaken idea that faith means telling everyone else how they should pray, eat, make love and celebrate life, and even what day and time to do it on.

Perhaps it's just the way we've evolved, but for a very long time in our human story, we've marched onto battlefields, certainty pumping through our veins, clinging to our symbol of divine support for whatever one-dimensional dogmatic polarity we're imprisoned in, to impose our particular idea of God's will on any number of infidels and ram our beliefs as far down one another's throats as we can reach.

To imagine that this activity has anything to do with either genuine faith or the divine is delusion of the highest order. It does, however, have everything to do with politics, power in service of the ego and simple human greed. And it's time we moved on. Wanting to share our good fortune with those we believe to be less fortunate is a beautiful thing. But thinking that we must impose our idea of God's gender, colour, laws and rituals on others just limits our potential access to the limitless. And if we truly have faith in our experience, we'll have no need to impose it on anyone.

From a shamanic perspective, God is what Anna in the beautiful book *Mr God, This is Anna* called 'an infinite number of viewing points'. Our experience of the divine is exactly and precisely who we are. Nothing more, nothing less. For shamans the world over, the divine is both right here with us in physical form in nature and out as far as the spirit can travel at the very edge of this expanding universe. It is the massive generosity of the Great Mother under our feet. It is visible in the murmuration of a flock of swallows. It is the melody of a stream and the mystery of a shooting star. It is everywhere and everything. It is beyond polarity. It is the creative embrace of opposites. And in these times, when people and ideas are continuing to polarize, to the devastating detriment of the fabric of life, the connection to the one power in us and beyond us that can alchemize all apparent opposites into one magnificent unity seems to me to be needed more than ever.

I know that there is a thirst in me that can only be quenched by the waters from this oasis. In our last chapters, I'll invite you to be in dialogue with the divine so that you too can discover and deepen your access to this refuge, learn more about who you are and, like any Inner Shaman worth their salt, commit fully to serving life.

CHAPTER 14

Fulfilment

Your Life as a Shamanic Journey

*'Wherever there is a suitable environment for
the fulfilment of Life, it will fulfil itself.'*

JIDDU KRISHNAMURTI

The heart of a shaman's life is in the integrity of their relationships –
with themselves; with others, one to one; with their community,
ranging from their local plants, minerals and animals to the web of life
across the planet and out into the universe; with the imaginal world,
including their ancestors, descendants, spirits and allies; and with the
Great Spirit. For the shaman, fulfilment isn't just personal, it's based
on their love for life and commitment to all life.

Susannah and I and David Tucker, a dear friend, once took a group of
people to visit Sumpa, the Achuar elder shaman who we visited earlier
in our journey, just a few weeks after his wife of more than 60 years
had passed away. He was deeply sad, but he took the time to thank us
for coming to see him. He told us that the healing he would be offering

us would be the best medicine for his own broken heart. He proceeded to work with every single one of the 20 members of the group with exquisite care and attention. The next morning he told us, with tears in his eyes, that our visit and the opportunity to offer us healing had reminded him that he still had a reason to live.

For the shaman, finding fulfilment means serving life from the deepest place within. In the modern world, it means not only having the precision of a clear mind and the ability to think critically and challenge the limitations of their own perception and knowledge, but also having a well-developed kinaesthetic and emotional intelligence. Shamans are able to move safely between the imaginal and physical worlds because of their strong connection to both. And the result of that connection is that even the most basic of everyday tasks can be infused with the magic of ritual.

The different stages of shamanic training are marked by initiations. An initiation is a ritual designed to mark significant change. A good initiation takes us out of our comfort zone. It puts us in a situation where we have to find a new level of humility, strength and connection to a higher power in order to survive. It also gives us the chance to reveal what we have learned to our elders and community and to be recognized by them – an aspect of community that is highly valued by the indigenous communities we know.

In the modern world, life in its wisdom gives us many challenges that we can learn to recognize as initiations. Moving from childhood to puberty and adolescence, committing to a relationship, becoming a parent, losing close family or friends, moving to a new home or job, turning 50, going through the menopause and becoming a grandparent are just some of the moments that can benefit from the focus and prayer that initiation rituals can provide.

Sadly, one of the things we have lost in the modern world is the art of initiation. And if you want to know the result of generation upon generation of young people going through adolescence without being initiated, just turn the news on any day of the week.

When our son was 13, we put him through an initiation. He said goodbye to his mama, who was going to visit a friend for 24 hours. As she left, he told her that he didn't want her not to be his mama anymore. She told him she would always be his mother but when she returned, she would no longer be the mother of a child but of a young man. She left him with me and seven men he had known all his life and had invited to be there. The initiation we had planned for him involved him spending four hours sitting in a circle of stones in the darkness, contemplating questions we had given him about the best and the most difficult times in his life. When he returned, he had to present his answers to us. He was then acknowledged as a young man and we had a great feast to celebrate. It was a simple ceremony, but one in which he had to find inner resources that up until then he didn't know he had.

If our elders don't initiate us, we have to find ways of doing it for ourselves. The fantastically anarchic and self-organizing rave scene of the 1980s was a perfect example. In the UK alone, more than a million teenagers every weekend went out in search of initiation. They danced all night, ecstasy fuelled and love driven. Complete strangers gave each other what friends and family couldn't – the solid gold of a moment of genuine recognition.

'I see you! You're alright, mate.'

'Yep! And so are you.'

Every connection that was made heightened the euphoria until that circle was so strong it lifted everybody up. 'I am a worthless nobody' was transformed into 'I am part of something incandescent and irrepressible. I belong to this "we" and it's bigger than "me". It's filled with a power of love I never knew existed. Whoever you are, wherever you're from, whatever you're on, I'm with you and you're with me and we're alright.'

And so it went, weekend after weekend. And how did society respond? Did we go to our community shamans and respected elders and ask them what this outburst of uncontrollable joy and self-discovery was? Did we recognize the genuine need that was being expressed and enquire into how we could make it safe for everyone and genuinely beneficial for us all?

No. We made it illegal and tried to close it down.

I'm not talking about the pros and cons of drugs here, I'm talking about the genuine need for rituals and initiations that take us past our everyday selves. That stretch us beyond our known limits and show us what we are capable of. I'm talking about rituals that open up spaces where we can discover prayer that's physical and real because it's coming from so deep inside us that all we can do is get out of the way. Rituals that transport us into a genuine connection with the wider community that we belong to and inspire us to make our contribution. So that when Monday morning comes, we're not depressed because we're facing a life that feels empty and meaningless. We're inspired because we know who we are and what's ours to contribute. Any society that replaces guided initiations for its adolescents with smartphones and nature deficit disorder is asking for trouble.

Whatever our age, the next initiation is never far away. As the seasons turn and the years go by, the more we become who we are, the stronger we will be, the more impact we will have, and therefore the more responsibility we will have to take for our choices. But as we grow in our practice, we'll start to trust ourselves and the powers that guide us more. If your journey with trust is anything like mine, you'll become more and more aware that life is the master and the best we can do is dance and be as creative as we can with whatever it brings.

THE NINE LIFE CYCLES

In our Movement Medicine work, inspired by Gabrielle Roth's Cycles work which we taught for more than a decade, we see the whole journey of life from birth to death as an initiatory journey through nine developmental cycles, each with its own archetypal teacher and task. The nine life cycles describe the archetypal development of the human soul and are also a very useful map for developing any creative project. Any new idea needs a good mama to receive it, see its beauty and nourish it so that it can grow. You know now that we tend to repeat the stories from the past that have not yet been digested. Incarnation can be quite a process and how we began our journey in this life will continue to be echoed in all our beginnings until we do the work of digesting that original experience. The good news is that with the help of the Inner Shaman, we can do exactly that. Whoever our mama was or is, once we recognize that we can lean in to the support of the Great Mama under our feet, we can forgive, move on and embody the quality of healthy mothering that is a necessary part of any new beginning.

And once that baby project becomes a child, it will need a good archetypal papa to give it a strong hand at its back and say, 'Go on child, grow. Shine like the sun. Yes! Yes you can!'

Events in the present often catalyse us to re-experience events from the past that are unacknowledged or incomplete. When this happens, the Inner Shaman smiles. Though they recognize that there's work to be done and it's likely that all kinds of emotions will be bursting their banks, they also know that when we become conscious of what was previously hidden, we discover a rich vein of natural wealth in our psyche. We're all capable of using the stones on our path to build bridges, not walls. Though the cards we are dealt clearly make a difference to where we begin, we have a lot of choice about where we end up. As I have continued to work with the formative experiences of my early life, some of which have roots that go far back into my ancestors' experiences, more and more diamonds have become visible in the apparent darkness. Some of these are in the form of personal allies who have helped me at difficult moments in my life and have remained with me. I'm confident you'll discover that the same is true for you.

Each year Susannah and I run a nine-day course to work with the nine life cycles. It's called 'Initiation'. We take participants on a shamanic journey to extract medicine from the past, creating meaning from it that is grounded in self-acceptance and injecting a strong dose of dignity into their foundations. From there, with this newly discovered resilience at their back, they can see their lives afresh and dream a road ahead that is congruent with who they are and what really matters to them. The essential teachings that are the backbone of the course are the basis of a nine-day ritual that I'm going to invite you to do now.

🌿 PRACTICE: THE INNER SHAMAN'S 🌿 JOURNEY THOUGH THE NINE LIFE CYCLES

Being aware of the heroic journey you are on will strengthen your compassion for yourself and others and ultimately your capacity to bring your dreams to Earth by harnessing the raw material of your life experience. When a situation triggers you into reactivity, your Inner Shaman's capacity to stay steady and recognize who inside you has been triggered and what their story is will be a significant benefit to you.

This isn't about attempting to be a spiritually perfect human. It's about being real, kind and honest with yourself and others. In this way, the work that is yours to do will become visible and you'll be well on the way to enjoying the deepest fulfilment you can have in this life.

Timing

This is a powerful ritual and I'm going to suggest that you do it over nine consecutive days. An hour a day will suffice. Since it can be catalytic, you may wish to place some extra support in place. You could ask a friend to be with you and even do the work together, side by side. Remember the Dancing Warrior knows when they need help.

Preparation

 ✎ Look over the nine life cycles map below. It describes the journey we are all on. Note which cycle you are in and what is touched within you as you consider its archetypal teachers and initiatory tasks and opportunities. Every time I do this, I discover something new.

Number	Cycle	Archetypal teacher	Task/opportunity
1	Conception/ gestation	The Great Mystery	Incarnation and coming to Earth
2	Birth/ babyhood	The Mother/ Earth Mother/ Divine Mother	Connection with the mother, the body and learning to receive
3	Childhood	The Father/ Sun Father/ Divine Father	Connection with the father, friendship, play and learning about structure
4	Puberty (innocence)	The Nascent Self/ The Dreamer	Being recognized, welcomed and initiated as an individual in the community
5	Adolescence	The Edge-Walker	Individuation and experimentation
6	Adulthood	The Personal Dreamer (*)	Responsibility, family and work
7	Maturity	The Sacred Dreamer (•)	Self-knowledge, contributing what you have and harvest
8	Elderhood	The Master	Fulfilment, sharing wisdom and Benevolent Death, retiring from the world
9	Gateway to Death	The Great Mystery	Letting go, realization and surrender to Benevolent Death

(*) The personal dream is taking care of the foundations of life: work and finances, and family if that is part of your journey.

(•) The sacred dream is what you are here for: your purpose, your offering, your bliss.

Practice

I suggest that you work with each cycle in order, beginning with incarnation and ending with Death. Each day, work with one cycle as follows:

- Name the cycle and your intention to learn as much as you can from it.

- Set up your space in the normal way with as much focus and attention to detail as you can. How we begin a journey makes a big difference to the quality of that journey and where it can take us.

- Arrive at the centre of your circle and connect to your resources, using any of the foundational practices. Make sure your body is warm, joints mobile, breath deep and steady and your Inner Shaman and their medicine present. Remember that emotion means energy in motion and welcome your heart and its intelligence into this ritual.

- If you are working with a cycle you have already lived through, turn around, look at the road that has brought you here and be present, rooted and resourced at the centre of your circle.

- If you are working with a future life cycle, imagine the path of your life unfolding in front of you.

- Give your attention to the cycle and acknowledge your current relationship to it. How does it feel in your body and heart? When working with the past, what stories do you have about what happened in that cycle? When working with the future, what is the best outcome you can dream for that cycle?

- Invoke the archetypal teacher associated with the cycle to work alongside your Inner Shaman and all their helpers. This is the Unbroken energy that will help you to heal the wounds caused by your experiences. For instance, if you had a difficult relationship with either or both of your parents or guardians, the Mother/Father archetypes can help you to feel the Earth under your feet and the sun in your heart and receive *now* whatever you didn't receive *then*. For the Inner Shaman, blame and emotions associated with the past are there to be expressed and are temporary. Lessons learned from the past are permanent.

✐ Once you feel the presence of the cycle's archetype, step back into that cycle as the Inner Shaman, taking all your medicine with you. As you know through your work with the *SEER Process*, you have the resources to change your relationship to the past and the meaning you have taken from it.

✐ Acknowledge, express and release what you find:

~ Through connecting directly to the medicine of the archetypes and sending that back across the arc of time.

~ Through calling those parts of your inner community that feel lost in the frozen landscapes of the past into the warmth and protection of your heart. Embrace them and welcome them home.

If you ever find yourself overwhelmed, you're going too fast. Slow down. Breathe. Step back into the present, ground yourself in your moving body and continue with less intensity.

✐ When you feel your work with the cycle is complete, ask:

~ 'What lesson can I take from this cycle to support myself in my present situation?'

~ 'What help was present for me at that time that I was unaware of? Are there any allies who wish to make themselves known and become part of my personal mesa and bring more spiritual strength to my backbone?'

✐ Take the time to notice how present the archetype associated with each cycle is for you. Embody them and invite them to share their perspective. All these archetypes can become a helpful part of your inner community.

🖋 Consider your relationship to the initiatory task of the cycle.

🖋 Once you reach the cycle you're currently in, acknowledge how far you've come. It's really important to celebrate your success as well as acknowledge the work to be done. Ask yourself:

～ 'How am I doing with my personal dream and with taking responsibility for my life?'

～ 'How am I with my sacred dream?'

🖋 You can now look forward to the cycles that are ahead of you. Step forward into your future. Dream an unfurling road that inspires you and includes your relationships with yourself, others, your community and your allies.

🖋 Once you've spent time with all nine cycles, their archetypes and tasks, step back into the middle of your circle. Imagine all these parts of your inner community around you. From the central perspective of the Inner Shaman, sit in council with them and ask if any of them have anything more they wish to communicate.

🖋 Complete your work each day in the normal way, remembering to thank and release all you have called. Take some rest and digestion time, find an incantation that distils the essence of your work and take a simple step that is congruent with what you have done.

🖋 When you get to the end of the final day, take some extra time to bring together all your incantations and all you have learned and give thanks for this rich harvest of your life's experiences and the dreams you have for the road ahead.

☘☘☘☘

Congratulations! The work you have just done has been a powerful step towards fulfilling the unique blueprint of your soul.

Whenever I do a healing, I always ask the patient to plant a tree so that the benefit of the healing can go on growing through the seasons and bring blessings to others in the present and the future. I suggest that you find something to give that honours what you have received and is appropriate to your circumstances. Nothing is too small. Everything matters.

CHAPTER 15

The Infinite Well

The Inner Shaman's Relationship to Source

'The only people for me are the mad ones, the ones who are mad to live, mad to talk, mad to be saved, desirous of everything at the same time, the ones who never yawn or say a commonplace thing, but burn, burn, burn like fabulous yellow roman candles exploding like spiders across the stars.'

JACK KEROUAC

For the Inner Shaman, a good harvest involves experiencing an ever-deepening connection to self, others, the physical world, the imaginal world and the Great Mystery that is behind it all. I call this place of connection to the divine *the infinite well*, and it is where I go, alone or with others, to nourish myself and find the resilience and courage to return and face the music with a spring in my step, a tear in my eye and a smile that is soul deep.

Every ritual we've done has the potential to take you to this place. But the most reliable way I know of getting there is surrendering to the power of the rhythms of the drum. It doesn't matter whether we think we can dance or not. I believe that anyone in a body, no matter what its shape or fluidity, can dance past their self-conscious self and into the unpredictable brilliance of their embodied soul.

When I first danced, I had no idea this was possible. But I have discovered time and time again that no matter where we begin or who we think we are, if we are willing, it only takes a relatively short time to dance past disbelief. Yes, it can be embarrassingly uncomfortable for a while. But the dance is a mistress of seduction. And rhythm is uncompromising. When I really dance, I stop caring about what I look like. The question of whether my dance is right or wrong, or my body the right shape, become distant nightmares. My emotions run free like a herd of wild horses released from captivity. And for a blessed few minutes, my mind becomes still. And that's when the door opens. For a time, as my body lets go, I can disappear in the dance and open my heart to the Creator. In that space, there is nowhere to hide and there is nothing to hide. I become transparent.

As I drink my fill at this infinite well, my gratitude often spills over in tears and laughter. There may be a humming silence inside the rhythm of the drums and I may watch my very human drama unfold with love, acceptance and compassion. When I return to the everyday world, my body spent and calm, that world is always a shade brighter than it was before.

This kind of peace is a power in itself and a huge resource. Genuine happiness and fulfilment remain a rare commodity in the modern world. With racism so rife and so much destruction of the natural world going on, with species extinction and climate change speeding up, and with levels of depression, obesity and mental illness rising in all areas of society, it can be hard not to be overwhelmed. I find myself needing to practise more, express my fears and furies and break through to the blessed waters of grief as often as I can. Grief isn't the same as self-pity. Tears that arise from feeling powerless are fear and anger disguised. Tears that arise from sorrow over what has been done and is being done to the world are rooted in love for life.

I don't feel weak when I let these waters flow. On the contrary, honest sorrow and the authentic joy of being alive are twins, and the one usually opens the door to the other. And it is through this gateway that I once again experience my connection to the Mystery.

When I was younger, I confess that I was a spiritual bypass junkie – I used my connection to a disembodied idea of the Great Mystery to protect myself from the pain of life and my own emotions. Now I know that genuine embodied connection to the Mystery is not the saccharine sweet blanket of a spiritual bypass, but a fierce power that illuminates everything and renders us wholly transparent and defenceless. When we can see ourselves through the eyes and heart of the Great Mystery, the power of peace is always close by. That kind of peace only comes through the heart. And rather than coming up with some bland spiritual ideal that suggests that everything is perfect as it is, it is the not knowing and the dissolving into that Mystery that gives me the strength to carry on.

Accepting uncertainty is a big part of this. It's taken me many years to find the optimal balance between the safety of certainty and the adventure of uncertainty. Without safety, we can be overwhelmed. Without risk, we can become static. Each of us needs to find that sweet spot where there is enough solid ground for us to be able to let go and trust that it's fine for what we know to be far outweighed by what we don't. And to be at peace with that. The most potent harvest of all my work is the ability to return to this embodied sense of the Great Spirit and to receive the power of peace it brings me. At the end of this chapter, I'll share with you the five-step practice that has helped me to enter into this relationship with the divine, whatever name you have for it.

But first I have a question for you.

❦ PRACTICE: DESIGN YOUR OWN RITUAL ❦ – WHAT IS IT YOU TRULY LONG FOR?

- Stop for a moment. Take a deep breath. As you breathe out, let your weight go.

- Sit down inside yourself. Relax. Remember that the Earth is holding you and everyone and everything you know. In all your joy and all your suffering, the Earth is holding the space for you to remember who you are.

- Take another breath. Draw in the sweetness of the breath of life. Can you feel the soft touch of the air on your skin? Can you hear the wind's song? Can you feel life saying, 'Go on, live!'?

- Take a moment to feel the waters of life inside you. Feel the ocean in your cells. Let a river run through you. Let rain wash your inner land clean. Relax into the deep blue sea of your heart.

- And feel the warmth of the sun's touch. Whatever the temperature outside, the sun is shining inside your trillion cells right now. Enjoy its kiss and, if you're in the mood, blow a kiss back.

- Feel your roots going deep down into the darkness of the ground. Feel the stability that comes from the love affair your physical body is having with gravity right now. It's a source of genuine strength.

✍ Reach up to the sky. Open your branches to the wide empty space above you. Take in that light as if it were the sweetest of medicines.

✍ Let your heart be supported by your roots while it unfurls its wings into the empty space above you. Feel how much space there is above you and how much ground below you. And experience that ground and empty space inside you.

✍ Okay. Good. Time for that question. Connect to your Inner Shaman and their resources and let them find their own words to ask: 'Universal intelligence, Great Spirit, Mystery of Life, will you please show me who I am and what it is I truly long for?'

✍ You can just ask the question, but at this stage, why not go ahead and design and set up your own ritual space in which to be with this question? Go on, you can do it. You have enough foundations now in your practice to ask that question from a genuinely empowered place. Be in your backbone, dignified in who you are. One of the deeper pleasures of my life is to ask questions whose answers only land once the mind has let go of everything it already knows.

✍ However you ask, stay with it for a while. A few minutes would be wonderful. The more relaxed you can be, the better. You may even like to ask the question as you fall asleep at night. That allows your dreaming self to show you more details, nuances and layers in the question, and for the answer to reveal itself step by step inside you.

Each night, as we sleep, we are given direct access to the university of intelligence that is our unconscious. Time and time again on my journey, the imagery of my dreams has revealed things that my waking self hasn't known.

For the Inner Shaman, dreaming is a whole practice in itself. Many wonderful books have been written on the subject, some of which you'll find in the Resources section. Dreaming is so useful because, simply put, when we sleep, our left brain sleeps, leaving our right brain free to party. When we become lucid in our dreams, right and left brain work together in a way that helps us to be conscious inside our own unconscious.

Ritual is an embodied pathway to much the same state of awareness. For that reason, I sometimes call it *dreaming awake*. The shamanic rituals I've been introducing you to have involved dancing past your everyday self and into a more embodied, heartful, right-brain kind of consciousness that gives you a much clearer view of the bigger picture of which you are a part.

✍ So, once you've asked your question, let go and listen to what comes. Don't worry if it takes a while. Just make time to be with the question. Hang out with it. Follow the golden thread of your enquiry into the wide open space of the unknown. Ask it until you know the answer in your bones, in your blood, in all five chambers of your heart, in your entire being, until it is a feeling in your body, a body that is so full of life that you may just have to get up and dance some more.

ξξξξ

Well done. The ongoing enquiry into knowing who you are and what you long for is an important aspect of transformation. It is vital to update your inner sense of who you are with each step on the journey you take. Not doing this is the biggest obstacle to progress that I see in my students. If you don't consciously update your self-talk, your old story can easily reassert its hold on your perception.

As I mentioned in the introduction to Part IV, in all the rituals I do I acknowledge and work with all of the Five Dimensions of Relationship. When I don't, something vital is left out.

Ongoing awareness of these dimensions enables us to both expand our understanding of ourselves and see our own existence in terms of the interconnectedness we have with all beings:

- In the First Dimension, relationship with self, we expand from a conditioned and unconscious self to become the artist of our own experience through the meaning we give it and the story we tell.

- In the Second Dimension, relationship with others, we expand from being separate and lonely to being with another person in an honest and mutually beneficial way, learning from each other and helping each other's soul to grow.

- In the Third Dimension, relationship with community, we expand from sleepwalking through virtual reality to remembering that we have something of value to give to the diverse web of life to which we belong.

- In the Fourth Dimension, relationship with the imaginal world, we expand from unconsciously using the power of our imagination to keep ourselves imprisoned in the known, to understanding the power of what we dream and turning that power towards what we wish to create.

- The first four dimensions act like four table legs, giving us the stability to enter the fifth. What we call the Fifth Dimension is the place to discover and deepen your relationship to the Source.

Shamans are cartographers of the imaginal world. They use their own healing journey to map the territory so that others can safely follow in their footsteps. Though there are universal experiences that appear across belief systems and cultures, as I have already mentioned, each and every individual's experience of the divine is unique to them. I'm going to invite your Inner Shaman to enter into a five-step enquiry that will help you to recognize and develop your relationship to this sanctuary. The first three steps are based on duality. There is you. And there is the Great Spirit. The fourth is the bridge and the fifth invites you to go beyond duality.

The five steps are:

1. South: Be present and reveal yourself to the Great Mystery

2. East: Connect and dialogue with the Mystery

3. West: Release and surrender to the Mystery

4. North: Open yourself to the shining light of the Mystery

5. Centre: Dissolve into and become the Mystery

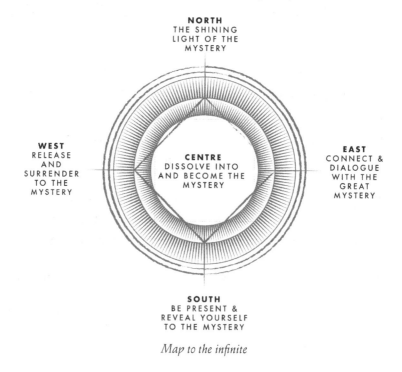

Map to the infinite

Before we begin, I want to emphasize one more time that you don't have to believe in the Great Spirit or anything else to do this practice. All you need is curiosity about the Mystery of life.

🌿 PRACTICE: A JOURNEY 🌿
TO THE INFINITE WELL

Timing

How far you wish to take this is up to you. Take as long as you like and take small steps if this is new to you, and build your confidence through practice.

Preparation

- Set up your space. Find or create an object that represents the Great Mystery and place it at the centre of your circle. It would also be helpful to place an object in each direction to represent the elements. Find the right music. Good music is an excellent ally in going past whatever resistance may arise. You can use a drum or a rattle or create a playlist that goes up and down in tempo.

- Call all that supports and guides you. Complete the *Awakening the Dancer* practice (p.29). Connect with the Inner Shaman and their allies. Move your body! Dance! All with the intention of entering into dialogue with the Great Spirit!

- It may be important for you to find ways to honour your tribal roots and the traditions you grew up with. I am in no way asking you to discount or ignore these. As part of my own journey, I have had to explain to my own ancestors why I have needed to move away from their traditions and find my own ways of being in connection with the source. As time has gone on, I have been able to integrate what I grew up with into what I have learned. Honouring our roots is important, so as you move, take the time to do so.

Practice

✍ Okay, when you are ready, I suggest you very simply move through the first four dimensions:

~ Acknowledge where you are in relationship with yourself.

~ Bring the people you love into your heart and your breathing, your moving. Offer your dance on behalf of them.

~ Expand to offer your dance and make an offering, a prayer on behalf of your community – both your local community and the places and situations in the world to which you feel connected.

~ Welcome your spirits, ancestors and descendants and offer your dance on behalf of them. Invite the spirit of the dance to move through your dance.

✍ And now open your awareness to the Great Spirit. Feel it as a tangible presence through the life moving through your body.

✍ Continue by stepping into the South of your circle. Dance yourself into the foundations of your relationship with God. Reveal yourself. You are who you are. And you can ask the Great Mystery anything and tell the Great Mystery everything. Simply let your heart say what it wants to say. In my experience, you cannot offend the Great Mystery. Say it in movement. Say it in words. Say it in sound and song. Say it with your whole being.

✍ Having revealed and expressed yourself, step into the East and the Fire. Imagine the Great Spirit is present. Now, here's a leap for your imagination: take a little time to see yourself from the point of view of the Great Spirit. What does this human need to know from you? Write them a personal letter that they can read later. Enjoy your time as the Great Spirit looking at your human self before returning to that self. Then take a moment to receive whatever this 'channelling of the source' gave to you and say whatever you need to complete this dialogue for now.

- Now step into the Waters. This is the place to let old ideas, feelings and stories in your relationship with the Great Spirit be washed away. Surrender yourself to the rhythm. Let a storm blow through you. Like a butterfly about to emerge from a chrysalis, shake from the inside out and let your old skin crack open and be washed away by the waters of life. Release everything that arises in your relationship to this Great Mystery. Nothing's too small. Imagine the rhythm is the very essence of the Mystery cleansing you, emptying you until there is nothing left.

- Now step into the North. Let yourself dance into that hollow bone state and ask for a new vision of the Great Mystery to blow in on the wings of your imagination. Dance like Zorba. Dance like a dervish. Dance like you've never danced before and pray for a vision. Feel the Great Spirit as the breath of life. Receive it. Receive a new vision. It may be just a seed now, but it will grow into the next stage of your relationship with the Mystery.

- Finally, step into the centre. There is nothing to do here but be, breathe, dissolve and let go. Resting may well be enough. Let your Inner Shaman guide you. And take as much time as you can here in the infinite well, dissolving, disappearing and then witnessing how you reconstruct your self and your world as you return.

- Make a few notes about your experience.

- Think of one simple action you can take in the days to come that will help you to know that you are integrating this ritual.

- Dedicate the medicine of your ceremony to whatever you wish to.

- And then thank and release all you have danced with.

- Rest in the silence and the echo of your work.

Return often to this infinite well. The more personal you allow your relationship with the Great Mystery to become, the easier it becomes to notice and connect to the infinite number of forms it takes.

☙☙☙☙

For the Inner Shaman, the Great Spirit is everything. Wherever we look and wherever we don't, the unexplainable and ever-changing fractals of consciousness that carry the fingerprint of the Great Spirit look right back at us. In some places it's obvious and in others it's anything but. But look hard enough and breathe deeply enough and the infinite will welcome you into the shining black light of its embrace and you will remember who you are.

CHAPTER 16

Brunch with the Great Spirit
Shamanic Death and Rebirth

*'I see a time of Seven Generations when all the colors
of mankind will gather under the Sacred Tree of Life
and the whole Earth will become One Circle again.'*

CRAZY HORSE

The perspective of the Fifth Dimension isn't the only truth. Nor is it the best truth. Nevertheless, it puts all other perspectives in their proper place. The Fifth Dimension can't be colonized or owned by any religion or belief system, but it contains them all. It incorporates all suffering and all joy. It is the home of the all-enveloping embrace of the Great Mystery and it is always everywhere. Entry to it is usually preceded by a death of some kind. Most recently for me, it involved the death of a belief system that I'd been carrying in my cells since my first few weeks of life.

I'd been under a lot of pressure. Writing this book alongside all that was happening in the world had been a genuine threshing. The grain of my experience and the practices I wanted to share had been separated from their husks by the ritual of writing. At one point, I genuinely felt that I might be losing my marbles. Everything was making me cry. Not just a few teardrops, but at times an uncontrollable torrent. I felt pressure building up inside me. I felt a connection through my father's line to all the men who hadn't known how and when to ask for help. I'm not someone who worries about himself a lot. I know my strength, but at that point I became genuinely concerned that my heart couldn't manage the stretch. I know it sounds dramatic, and it was. I was out of control in a way I hadn't been for more than 30 years. That breakthrough had opened the door to the adventure that had led me to where I was. Who knew where this one would take me?

Benevolent Death came into the room. I had entered a spontaneous ritual.

Benevolent Death asked me, 'What is ready to die?'

Through the breaking waves of emotion, I told Death that I'd always kept a part of my heart hidden. When I had been very young, when this world had felt unbearably raw and bleak I had survived by keeping a part of my essence in the spirit world, protected by my guardian angel. This had become my number one survival strategy: retreating to that world and never really allowing myself to trust in the support of any human being. But now, through writing this book, I had agreed to bring another level of my medicine to Earth and I had to recognize I couldn't do it alone. I needed support. I needed to trust. Shaking from this internal earthquake, my armour cracked and falling, I was standing at the edge of the known.

As I told Death why I was there, Death nodded slowly in reply and the door between the worlds opened in front of me. Through the storm, I felt that familiar feeling of everything beginning to fall away.

Once the door was fully open, I stepped through. There was a moment of quiet and focused intention. My last thought was one of gratitude for Susannah, who was sitting quietly by my side. I knew she would keep this space safe for me. Everything was taken care of and I could let go.

The *shamanic death* of totally letting go means encountering death while still alive. It means letting our individual form dissolve and merge with the Cosmos. It strips us naked. Don't invoke it if you wish to remain hidden from yourself. Or if you wish to present only half of your story. This is an all-or-nothing experience. But such a direct experience of the source gives us what I believe all of us are longing for. It reminds us, not in theory but in actuality, that we are love beyond imagination, that we are choosing the story we tell and that we are the universe getting to know itself through our experience – all of it, without exception.

We can't force this opportunity to present itself to us. But we can stack the cards by showing up often and presenting ourselves at this doorway between worlds. Every now and then the door will open, and when it does, we can leap through. So, come with me now, if you will. I'm about to skydive into the arms of the Mystery. Don't worry, all you need is to show up honestly, as you are, with the intention to learn. And repeating the practices I've shared with you on our journey together will have created enough structure and fluidity for you to have the possibility of experiencing the shamanic death of a total letting go and having the wherewithal to return, enriched beyond imagination, to continue your journey.

So, come, you are invited to take a little brunch with the Great Spirit.

🌿 PRACTICE: BRUNCH WITH THE GREAT SPIRIT 🌿

Call that Inner Shaman, and travel with me. Death has my heart in their hands and I hear my heart's rhythm pulsing through the ocean of my blood. I know that this door opens rarely and there's always fear when it does. But I see the edge of infinity and, as Don Juan said, infinity stares back at me, impassive and open.

Ready? Come with me now. Step off this edge with me and fall.

Okay? The rhythm is very fast and very steady, and the chants and drums of our people are all around us. The pulse of form and formless is already unwrapping muscle from bone, releasing spirit from flesh. Very soon, through the swirling tunnels of universal mind, everything will begin to dissolve. We are already stripped of solid form. There is nobody here to feel afraid or to feel pain, there is simply an echoing infinity of everything and nothing embracing as this Universal Consciousness dreams itself through all things and finds out just exactly who it is. Here all time is happening at once, yet we are beyond time. There is only this. All polarities and dualities have dissolved back into the infinite ocean from which they were born. Pulse. Silence. Everything. Nothing. Silence. Pulse. Forever.

We've been here before, you and I. We were here at the beginning. We will be here at the end.

We are dreaming and we are totally awake.

The pulse continues. We are geometric perfection dancing in and out of form. We are inside the tiniest tear and the sweetest smile. We are inside all cries of agony and ecstasy, of remembering and forgetting. Every note and every impossible piece of artistry is present. There is death of every kind and we are there inside all of it as killer and killed. And there is life of every kind and all that is yet to be imagined. All polarities arise here. We are the blackest light that shines. We are everything inside everything. *Everything.* Here, everything is everything.

This door between worlds is always open. There is always going and returning, and returning is being reborn. The pulse turns everything back into something. And the something recognizes itself as a wave, or a fractal of a flame. An invisible breath of Air breaks free to be itself and a form that is a body welcomes the travelling spirit home. There is a long time of falling back into infinity and returning to self. From this perspective, all the Five Dimensions of Relationship are the universal source getting to know itself.

And we are not alone. We never have been. And we never will be. We support and we are supported. It's as easy as breathing. In. Out. In. Out.

So here we are, back in this world. There's no feeling of loss when we return. Gratitude doesn't even begin to cover it.

Imagine you have chosen to be here on this Earth. Imagine you love life in a body. Imagine you love the creativity in duality and polarity. Yes, there is trouble here. Lots of it. Mostly because we've forgotten that we are family. Every single one of us comes from the same place. Dissolving reminds me of this. It reminds me that I, you and all things are here to play our role in the full knowledge that we are all just the universe getting to know itself through us. This is about as real as reality gets. And I love it because it stops me taking myself and my identities, roles and ideas too seriously. And that frees the shamanic artist in me to take everything that life brings as an invitation to create.

Here we are now. Returned from our journey and fully embodied. Everything is the same and everything has changed. Our presence is required. There is work to be done. There is medicine to share. The jewel of our soul wants to know itself and be known. Let's see what we can discover today. Let's see what we can create. Body breathing. Spirit and matter as one.

My elders tell me that after returning from any journey like this, it's a good thing to share our experience with people who want to know us as we are. In the experiencing and the sharing, we own and become the medicine we have discovered. Your Inner Shaman is so ready to help you do this. And I trust them and I trust your medicine. All your allies and guardians and, most importantly, your experience of connection through your body to the life that lives it, are the umbilical cord that connects your imaginal and physical worlds, your dream and its manifestation.

This is the gig here for all of us: total commitment to being who we are. Total commitment to burning as brightly as we can until there is nothing left of our body but dust. As for the spirit, who knows where that is headed? That's why the Great Mystery is my master. That Mystery knows how to keep a secret and hide it in plain sight.

Epilogue

*'I want to stand by the river in my finest dress. I want
to sing strong and hard and stomp my feet with
100 others so that the waters hum with our happiness.
I want to dance for the renewal of the world.'*

ROBIN WALL KIMMERER, *BRAIDING SWEETGRASS*

In the end, there is only the practice of presence. So, whenever you feel it's the right moment again, make sure you are safe and have everything you need. And then call everything that supports you and tell the Great Spirit who you are. Enter into dialogue with it. Surrender to what's true. Let it all move through you. Expand and fall off the edge of yourself. Be totally embraced. Dissolve until there's nothing left but everything. Then, when you're ready, return, refreshed, renewed, resourced and held in the infinite embrace of the Mystery.

Discovering what matters to us and finding a way to bring it to Earth as our offering – this is the shaman's way. When we are ourselves and do something purposeful with the gift of life we have been given, we make life sacred. Dedicate yourself every day to what is true for you, to what is true inside you. Your Inner Shaman knows the love that exists between spirit and matter, between the Earth and the Mystery that has transformed it from a cauldron of boiling matter into everything your eyes can see, your ears can hear and your heart can feel. Your Inner Shaman is awake inside the miracle of the Mystery and is connected to everything that you need to bring what you dream to Earth. For yourself and for all your relations.

The possibility that the best outcome of our evolution we are capable of dreaming is where we have got to now breaks my heart. Is that really the best we can do with our brilliant creativity? Is that really what we want? To be separate in hermetically sealed units, our bodies spreading sideways as we lose touch with the wild majesty of nature and the infinite intelligence of the universe?

Our only problems are a lack of imagination and the belief that this doesn't matter. That we don't matter. Our challenge is to dream up a more compelling and inspiring purpose than settling for a dream that only serves a tiny part of who we are. We can do better than selling our soul for more and more useless pap. While we can, even should this turn out to be our last sunset, let's open our eyes. Let's taste life. Let's seek out that smile inside our belly that comes from knowing who we are. So that when death comes, we can open our arms wide, breathe out and let our last breath be our sweetest yet.

The Inner Shaman knows that the real wealth of our lives lands when we risk connecting – with ourselves, with another person, with community and with what we dream. Failures along the road are inevitable and being too concerned with outcomes gets in the way. So we need to do what makes sense to us regardless of the outcome. The Inner Shaman is there to play their role. Nothing more. And nothing less.

To evolve with nature, to join forces with it, we also have to remember that life has its own timing. Sometimes evolution is quick. Sometimes it is slow. Living fast is fun, but not all of the time. As I'm getting older, my relationship with time is changing. Now, things often come around and pass too quickly. The sands of time are slipping through my fingers and there's nothing I can do to stop them. Except be present. Because when I am, when I'm listening and connected, things always happen in good time. The deepest prayer I know is that our will aligns with the will of the Great Spirit. When that happens, we can rest in the arms of the Great Mystery and enjoy the ride.

Everything makes a difference. And everything matters. Interoception. Setting boundaries. Listening. Communicating. Receiving. Giving back. Remembering our ancestors, spirits and descendants. Relating across all the Five Dimensions of life. Though there will always be rough waters to cross, peace will always descend again, like the velvet calm of the night. Now that you're finished, it's time to begin. I suggest you start again with Awakening the Dancer, and go through all the rituals again.

Michael Harner, a respected elder in the shamanic community, said, 'Shamanism is being re-invented in the West precisely because it is needed.' I have every faith that the ancient archetype of the Inner Shaman, reinvented to meet and match who you are, will be a good guide for you should you choose to listen to them. This book is a purposeful invocation of the power and deep connectivity of the Shaman in you. This offering is one more leaf on the Tree of Life.

I believe that our species will continue to evolve and I pray that we will learn to bring together the best of all wisdom and all medicine for the wellbeing of all our relations.

May you always find all that you need to go on being who you are and giving all you've got. You have so much to give. And, as environmentalist Wes Jackson said, 'If your life's work can be accomplished in your lifetime, you're not thinking big enough.'

See you at the door between all worlds. There's no more potent place to be. And no more potent time than now. We've reached the end and the end is another crossroads. You could put this down and get distracted again. Or you could stand up and stomp your feet 'and dance for the renewal of the world.'

We either wake up to this magnificent chance we have to make a difference. Or we curl up and crawl back into our mediocrity. We either recognize the power of our imaginations and put them in service of a more conscious dream. Or we go back to sleep and carry on complaining about the people who should be doing it better. The Inner Shaman knows who you are and what that life force that's beating your heart right now is capable of. And they know that the life of future generations is in all of our hands. They grieve for what we've lost, but they remain full of gratitude for the strong-hearted and courageous dreams of what we yet might create.

From the shaman in me to the shaman in you. May the sun rise in your heart tomorrow morning and every morning before you die. And may the moon bring you dreams that remind you of what matters most.

Tick Tock! Tick Tock!

End.

Begin again.

Entheogens

There are many ways of meeting the divine. And though they are absolutely not part of Movement Medicine practice or the practices I am offering you in this book, it would be remiss of me to write a book about shamanism and not say a word about entheogens.

Entheogens are plant medicines known for their capacity to take us over the edge of surrender and into a direct experience of the divine. Despite the fact that they are usually illegal in the modern world (apparently we're not able to make informed decisions for ourselves), they are everywhere. And if you're interested enough in shamanism to have read this far, you're likely to meet them somewhere along the road. They are usually offered in a shamanic context, although they are just one form of shamanic practice. Since there's no doubt that at the right time, in the right place, with the right intention, in an impeccably held space, they can be helpful for people, here's my view on them.

First and foremost, though it's likely you'll meet people who'll tell you all kinds of things about how plant medicines have helped them, never let anyone persuade you to do something against your will or your better judgement. If you feel any fear, pay attention to it. Fear isn't a disease, it's a call to pay attention in the face of something that may appear to be a threat to your wellbeing. There is no medicine that's good for everyone and discovering who YOU are is the intention of shamanic practice. In my experience, though plant medicines can reveal the inner and outer work that we need to do for that, they can't do the work for us. Hanging out in ecstatic states can be deeply resourcing, but when we return, our ego and unconscious will still be waiting for us. There's no way to bypass the biographical work we need to do if we wish to know who we are and be as effective as we can be in all areas of our life.

Having said that, humans have always sought the change of state that entheogens bring, and they always will. So, it would be sensible to learn from our indigenous friends how to integrate these kinds of experiences into society. Making them illegal just leads to more unsafe spaces and resultant casualties. Just like all the things the industrial culture embraces, plant medicines are often over-consumed by people who mistake the medicine for the destination rather than the path. And often, people take them without any awareness of their original context.

Ayahuasca, for instance, is part of a tradition that is at least 5,000 years old, originating in the Amazon. Many Amazon tribes have now concluded that they need to share their medicine with us so that we can experience what is part of their everyday knowledge: that the Earth is alive. That the forests are sacred temples of biodiversity. And that to go on destroying them is sacrilege on a grand scale. The indigenous peoples are sharing their medicine with the intention that these rituals will wake us up to the work we need to do together to preserve the lungs of the Earth for future generations. If you or anyone you know is working with this medicine and is unaware of this implicit request for support, please remind them about the law of reciprocity that is woven into ancient traditions. At the moment, in keeping with our consumer culture, we are taking way more than we are giving back.

Ayahuasca is said to be the vehicle through which the living intelligence or the spirit of the forest can communicate with us. Traditionally, it is used as part of an initiatory journey that helps people discover more about their role in life. In Achuar or Sápara territory, if not training to be a shaman, people normally only participate in three to five ceremonies during their entire lives. Once a vision has been received, the work begins. Our indigenous friends have told us that they don't seek out more visions until they have manifested the ones they've been given. Beware of the tendency to become vision junkies. Our underlying story of 'not enough-ness' supports our addictions, not our freedom, and we can easily apply those addictions to plant medicine.

As well as ayahuasca, there are many other entheogens on offer, some of them offered by people who have been trained in a living tradition, some by people who believe they've been 'called' to do so. Please be careful. Fear of the unknown is natural and respectful. It will help to keep you alert. Get recommendations. Don't throw away your critical thinking. Use it before and after any ceremony or ritual. Make sure you are safe. And then, if it's your informed choice to do so, take a running leap and enjoy the ride. Afterwards, make sure that you find a way to give back to whatever culture or tradition you have been working in; make full use of your experiences and find ways to integrate them into every area of your life.

Resources

Ya'Acov and Susannah Darling Khan

For access to all the work I offer: www.darlingkhan.com

Our online shamanic courses and ongoing online study through our membership site community: www.21Gratitudes.com

To find the people in your area who we have trained in Movement Medicine: www.movementmedicineassociation.org

Workshops, apprenticeship and training in Movement Medicine:
www.schoolofmovementmedicine.com
www.movementmedicineassociation.org

Shamans and Elders

If you discover, as I'm certain you will, that the Inner Shaman takes you deeper into your own power, purpose and passion to serve life, you'll need to find teachers and elders. Make sure that they are still learning, they know about safety and they aren't afraid to challenge you.

Shamans work with power. There's no way they can fulfil their role without it. Their training is focused on developing personal mastery. But, just as there are all kinds of artists, lawyer and politicians, there are all kinds of shamans. How trustworthy they are depends largely on what power they have and what they choose to use it for.

If you ever run into a shaman and want to get a sense of whether they are a good person to work with, here's a little checklist:

- Trust your interoception. Your animal self knows.

- Remember they are human just like you. And just like you, they will certainly have their blind spots.

- Do you see humility alongside power?

- Consider how they treat the people around them. Are those people blossoming and coming into their own power?

- Trust yourself. If something doesn't feel right, it probably isn't.

Recommended Reading

Shakil Choudhury, *Deep Diversity: Overcoming Us vs Them*, Between the Lines, 2015

Guy Claxton, *Intelligence in the Flesh: Why Your Mind Needs Your Body Much More Than It Thinks*, Yale University Press, 2015

Julie Diamond, *Power: A User's Guide*, Belly Song, 2016

Jem Friar, *Choosing Happier: How to Be Happy Despite your Circumstances, History or Genes*, Imaginal, 2017

Temple Grandin and Catherine Johnson, *Animals in Translation: The Woman Who Thinks Like a Cow*, Bloomsbury, 2005

Rick Hanson, *Buddha's Brain: The Practical Neuroscience of Happiness, Love, and Wisdom*, New Harbinger, 2009

Arkan Lushwala, *The Time of the Black Jaguar: An Offering of Indigenous Wisdom for the Continuity of Life on Earth*, CreateSpace, 2012

—, *Deer and Thunder*, CreateSpace, 2018

Chris Lüttichau, *Calling Us Home: Find Your Path, your Balance and your Inner Strength*, Head of Zeus, 2017

Sergio Magaña, *The Toltec Secret: Dreaming Practices of the Ancient Mexicans*, Hay House, 2014

—, *Caves of Power*, Hay House, 2016

Charlie Morley, *Lucid Dreaming Made Easy: A Beginner's Guide to Waking Up in Your Dreams*, Hay House, 2018

Bessel Van der Kolk, *The Body Keeps the Score: Mind, Brain and Body in the Transformation of Trauma*, Allen Lane, 2014

Daan van Kampenhout, *The Tears of the Ancestors: Victims and Perpetrators in the Tribal Soul*, Zeig, Tucker & Theisen, 2008

Music

For music to support your practice, including guided journeys and drumming by Ya'Acov and Susannah Darling Khan:
https://music-medicine.co.uk

Trauma Therapy

- Eye Movement Desensitization and Reprocessing Therapy (EMDR)

- The Sensorimotor Psychotherapy Institute

These are both modern therapeutic practices that are particularly helpful for dealing with trauma.

Protecting the Amazon

- Amazon Watch: https://amazonwatch.org

- The Naku Project – a Sápara educational and healing centre in the Ecuadorian Amazon: www.naku.com.ec/web/index.php/en

- The Pachamama Alliance: www.pachamama.org

ABOUT THE AUTHOR

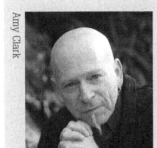

Ya'Acov Darling Khan is acknowledged as a practising shaman by indigenous elder shamans from the Arctic to the Amazon. He believes that a shift from society's focus on acquisition to reciprocity, a universal shamanic principal, is the key to repairing and evolving our connection to Self, each other and the biosphere on which we depend.

From an early age, Ya'Acov felt drawn to the invisible world of spirit that he sensed behind the physical world. A lightning strike on a golf course proved to be the awakening that changed the course of his life. It led to more than three decades of intense study and practice with indigenous and modern shamans from around the world.

Ya'Acov's teaching is inspiring, practical and directly from the heart. His audience includes people from all walks of life. He has taught on some of the most pre-eminent platforms driving the transformation of world culture and sustainability, including California's Esalen Institute and the Embodiment Conference. He founded Movement Medicine – an embodied, engaged shamanic practice for our times – with his wife, Susannah. The both teach worldwide and online.

Ya'Acov is the author of the bestselling *Jaguar in the Body, Butterfly in the Heart* and co-author, with Susannah, of *Movement Medicine*. He lives on an eco-smallholding with Susannah, their son, Reuben, and four Exmoor ponies.

www.darlingkhan.com

Listen. Learn. Transform.

Get unlimited access to over
30,000 hours of Hay House audio!

Today, life is more hectic than ever—so you deserve on-demand and on-the-go solutions that inspire growth, center your mind, and support your well-being.

Introducing the *Hay House Unlimited Audio* mobile app. Now, you can listen to the experts you trust and the titles you love—without having to restructure your day.

With your membership, you can:

- Enjoy over 30,000 hours of audio from your favorite authors.

- Explore audiobooks, meditations, Hay House Radio episodes, podcasts, and more.

- Listen anytime and anywhere with offline listening.

- Access exclusive audios you won't find anywhere else.

Try FREE for 7 days!

HAY HOUSE

Look within

Join the conversation about latest products,
events, exclusive offers and more.

 Hay House UK

 @HayHouseUK

 @hayhouseuk

 healyourlife.com

We'd love to hear from you!

Printed in the United States
By Bookmasters